D1479029

THE POETRY OF
Sir Philip Sidney

ENGLISH TEXTS AND STUDIES

GENERAL EDITOR: KENNETH MUIR

SIR PHILIP SIDNEY

THE POETRY OF
Sir Philip Sidney

An interpretation in the context of his life and times

J. G. NICHOLS

Principal Lecturer in English
Notre Dame College of Education
Liverpool

BARNES & NOBLE BOOKS
A Division of Harper & Row Publishers, Inc.

1974

Published in the U.S.A. 1974 by
HARPER & ROW PUBLISHERS, INC.
BARNES & NOBLE IMPORT DIVISION

Copyright © 1974 J. G. Nichols

Printed in England

ISBN 06 495163 4

First published 1974

Preface

Sidney is an approachable poet. The great personal charm attested by so many of his contemporaries is not something that we need to take on trust: it survives in his poems. In them the courtly manner he favoured is still winning without being ingratiating, still splendid without arrogance. Yet Sidney is not ultimately an easy poet. Textual problems and problems over the interpretation of details are not rare; but our chief difficulty is in being sure that we understand his intentions.

It sometimes seems that he is approachable in far too many ways. When is he serious, and when is he joking? When he is joking, as he often is, just how serious is the intention behind the humour? Above all, how seriously or solemnly should we take the protestations of love in *Astrophil and Stella*? Whose protestations are they anyway—Sidney's own or rather Astrophil's? It is with such questions that I am mainly concerned. Sir Philip may at times have worn his heart on his sleeve; but it was a stylized, emblematic heart on a well-cut, elegant sleeve, and the stylization and the quality of the cut were, I think, important to him and should be to us.

I first discuss Sidney's poetry in general in the light of his ideals and those of his age. This general discussion is followed by a consideration of the variety of ways in which *Astrophil and Stella* has been read. None of these ways, it seems to me, is satisfactory. The approach I suggest may be controversial, but it does answer the poetic facts.

Professor Kenneth Muir and Mr. R. T. Davies have encouraged me with their comments and criticism and enabled me to correct several errors of judgement. Those that may remain are my own.

I am indebted to Mrs. Alison M. Quinn who very kindly compiled the general and subject indexes to this work.

J.G.N.

This book was published with the aid of a grant from a
fund established by Mrs. S. A. Deakin in
memory of her son Arnold Davenport (1910–1958)
who was Andrew Cecil Bradley Senior Lecturer in the
Department of English Literature in the University
of Liverpool. Arnold Davenport was a distinguished
scholar in the field of Renaissance Studies and editor of
The Poems of Joseph Hall and *The Poems of*
John Marston, published in the Liverpool English
Texts and Studies series.

Contents

Abbreviations

Gentili   Vanna Gentili, ed. *Sir Philip Sidney: Astrophil and Stella.* 1965.

Kalstone   David Kalstone. *Sidney's Poetry: Contexts and Interpretations.* 1965.

Lever   J. W. Lever. *The Elizabethan Love Sonnet.* 1966 (first published 1956).

Montgomery   R. L. Montgomery. *Symmetry and Sense: The Poetry of Sir Philip Sidney.* 1961.

O.E.D.   *The Oxford English Dictionary.* 1961 (first published 1933).

Ringler   W. A. Ringler, ed. *The Poems of Sir Philip Sidney.* 1962.

R.S.V.   The Holy Bible, Revised Standard Version. 1961 (first published 1952).

Rudenstine   N. L. Rudenstine. *Sidney's Poetic Development.* 1967.

Shepherd   Geoffrey Shepherd, ed. *An Apology for Poetry.* 1965.

Spenser   *The Poetical Works of Edmund Spenser*, J. C. Smith and E. de Selincourt, eds. 1940 (first published 1912).

Tuve   Rosemond Tuve. *Elizabethan and Metaphysical Imagery.* 1965 (first edition 1947).

Young   R. B. Young. 'English Petrarke: A Study of Sidney's *Astrophel and Stella*', *Three Studies in the Renaissance: Sidney, Jonson, Milton.* 1958, pp. 5–88.

FOR GROUPS OF POEMS, AS IN RINGLER

O.A.   Poems from the *Old Arcadia.*

C.S.   *Certain Sonnets.*

A.S.   *Astrophil and Stella.*
O.P.   Other Poems.

PERIODICALS

C.L.   *Comparative Literature.*
E.A.   *Études Anglaises.*
E.L.H.   *Journal of English Literary History.*
H.L.B.   *Huntington Library Bulletin.*
H.L.Q.   *Huntington Library Quarterly.*
J.A.A.C.   *Journal of Aesthetics and Art Criticism.*
J.E.G.P.   *Journal of English and Germanic Philology.*
J.W.C.I.   *Journal of the Warburg and Courtauld Institutes.*
K.R.   *Kenyon Review.*
M.C.R.   *Melbourne Critical Review.*
M.L.N.   *Modern Language Notes.*
M.L.Q.   *Modern Language Quarterly.*
M.L.R.   *Modern Language Review.*
M.P.   *Modern Philology.*
N.Q.   *Notes and Queries.*
P.C.   *Poetry* (Chicago).
P.M.L.A.   *Publications of the Modern Language Association of America.*
P.Q.   *Philological Quarterly.*
R.E.S.   *Review of English Studies.*
R.N.   *Renaissance News.*
S.P.   *Studies in Philology.*
T.L.S.   *The Times Literary Supplement.*
T.S.E.   *Texas Studies in English.*

I

Words set in delightful proportion[1]

THE ELIZABETHAN POETS are renowned as metaphorical birds
of song with a fellow-feeling for that literal song-bird, the nightingale.[2] Sidney is no exception:

> The Nightingale, as soone as Aprill bringeth
> Unto her rested sense a perfect waking,
> While late bare earth, proud of new clothing springeth,
> Sings out her woes, a thorne her song-booke making:
>   And mournfully bewailing,
>   Her throate in tunes expresseth
>   What griefe her breast oppresseth,
> For *Thereus'* force on her chaste will prevailing.
>   O *Philomela* faire, ô take some gladnesse,
>   That here is juster cause of plaintfull sadnesse:
>   Thine earth now springs, mine fadeth,
>   Thy thorne without, my thorne my heart invadeth.[3]

Here is the customary Elizabethan melodiousness: the words seem
to beg to be set to music. They were, in fact, written for an
existing tune,[4] and were later set to at least one other.[5] There is
more in this poem, however, than a simple lyricism. With the
second stanza a fresh, and rather disturbing, element comes in as

---

1. Shepherd, p. 113.   2. Ringler, p. 427.   3. *C.S.* 4, ibid., p. 137.
4. The poem is headed '*To the same tune*', which refers to the preceding poem
(ibid., p. 136).
5. Ibid., p. 427. E. H. Fellowes, ed., *English Madrigal Verse 1588–1632*, revised
and enlarged by F. W. Sternfeld and David Greer, 1967, an anthology of madrigals
and lute-songs, contains seventeen poems by Sidney.

I

the plangent lament for the woes of nightingale and poet admits a
touch of gay and realistic wit:

> Alas she hath no other cause of anguish
> But *Thereus'* love, on her by strong hand wrokne,
> Wherein she suffring all her spirits' languish,
> Full womanlike complaines her will was brokne.
>> But I who dayly craving,
>> Cannot have to content me,
>> Have more cause to lament me,
>> Since wanting is more woe then too much having.
>>> O *Philomela* faire, ô take some gladnesse,
>>> That here is juster cause of plaintfull sadnesse:
>>> Thine earth now springs, mine fadeth,
>>> Thy thorne without, my thorne my heart invadeth.[6]

It must be small comfort for a victim of rape to be assured that
'wanting is more woe then too much having'. Clearly, we are meant
to think of the anguish, the witty anguish, of the frustrated lover
who speaks in this poem, rather than of any moral questions
raised by the rape of Philomela. Yet how does this fit in with
Sidney's central argument in his *Apology for Poetry* that the poet's
aim in writing is to make men 'know that goodness whereunto
they are moved'?[7]

Faced with this problem, a reader is likely at first to fall with
relief on a poem which seems to express its attitude simply and
clearly:

> Who doth desire that chaste his wife should be,
> First be he true, for truth doth truth deserve . . .[8]

This poem seems straightforward enough—a few pieces of sound
advice, saved from pomposity by the conciseness of the expression
and by the neat balance within each line and of one line with
another:

> Not toying kinde, nor causlesly unkinde,
> Not sturring thoughts, nor yet denying right,
> Not spying faults, nor in plaine errors blinde,
> Never hard hand, nor ever raines too light.

---

6. Ringler, p. 137. 7. Shepherd, p. 103. 8. *O.A.* 65, Ringler, p. 98.

More easily said (even so neatly said) than done perhaps. Then the husband who can manage to preserve the happy medium in so many different ways (and in a few other ways which I have not quoted) is told finally:

> This done, thou hast no more, but leave the rest
> To vertue, fortune, time and woman's brest.

'Thou hast no more.' Does this mean that the husband need do no more? In which case we wonder what more could be expected of any mortal. Or does it mean that it is not possible for him to do any more? This we are only too ready to believe. Moreover, the husband's helpers are not, on reflection, so reliable as the neat couplet in which they are mentioned might at first lead one to suppose. The previous poem in the *Old Arcadia*[9] to which this one is a reply has already shown lightheartedly how firm one woman's virtue was; fortune was proverbially 'blind', 'constant only in inconstancy' (a quality it shared with woman), 'fickle', and 'made of glass';[1] and anyone disposed to place any trust in 'woman's brest' should recall *inter alia* that 'Who has a woman has an eel by the tail'.[2] Time, of course, 'tries the truth'[3] and 'brings the truth to light',[4] a truth which we may suspect will come as a blow to this paragon of a husband. We should have been warned: the poem is spoken by Pas in reply to Nico, and these two have already tried to outdo each other's ingenuity in a singing- and slanging-match.[5]

It is all too easy, I think, to read Sidney's poetry too seriously, or rather too solemnly and too simply. The critic[6] who finds a lack of humour in Sidney's make-up is certainly a rare bird; but I suggest that, far from there being a danger in looking too hard for 'humour, irony, and detachment',[7] we may often easily fail to appreciate how subtle and sophisticated Sidney's art is.

The ninth sonnet in *Astrophil and Stella*[8] has come in for some hard words. The octave, with its comparison of Stella's face to the front of a building, has been described as 'a specimen of Sidney at

9. *O.A.* 64, ibid., p. 94.
1. M. P. Tilley, *A Dictionary of the Proverbs in England in the Sixteenth and Seventeenth Centuries*, 1950, p. 237.
2. Ibid., p. 742. See also pp. 743 and 745.   3. Ibid., p. 671.
4. Ibid., p. 670.   5. *O.A.* 29, Ringler, p. 51.
6. J. A. Symonds, *Sir Philip Sidney*, 1886, pp. 12–13.
7. As is suggested in T. W. Craik, *Sir Philip Sidney: Selected Poetry and Prose*, 1965, p. 10.
8. Ringler, p. 169.

his worst',[9] 'as crude as anything in the *Arcadia*',[1] and conventional even though well done.[2] The poem as a whole has been criticized as conventional and immature[3] or, more interestingly, as deliberately conventional with the aim of showing Astrophil's[4] immaturity as a lover at that stage in the sequence.[5] However, I do not think that we are meant to take the conventional manner of this sonnet, even when read without reference to the poems which surround it, quite so simply. It is not in such sharp contrast to other sonnets which criticize a conventional manner as has sometimes been made out.[6] It has been described as 'toneless',[7] and admittedly it does not contain such variety of tone as many of the sonnets in *Astrophil and Stella*; but surely there is a change of tone, a hint of mockery, in the second part of each of these two lines:

> Queene *Vertue's* court, which some call *Stella's* face,

and

> Whose porches rich (which name of cheekes endure).

The method is similar to that used in Sonnet 7, which has also been described as simply conventional:[8]

> When Nature made her chiefe worke, *Stella's* eyes . . .[9]

I am not suggesting that the praise of Stella in Sonnet 9 is intended ironically: it is very different from the poem by Alethes about Mopsa, in which she is compared (among other things)

---

9. E. C. Pettet, 'Sidney and the Cult of Romantic Love', *English*, vi (1946–7), 233.

1. Mona Wilson, *Sir Philip Sidney*, 1931, p. 172.

2. R. L. Montgomery, 'Reason, Passion, and Introspection in *Astrophel and Stella*', *T.S.E.* xxvi (1957), 128.

3. A. R. Howe, '*Astrophel and Stella*: "Why and How" ', *S.P.* lxi (1964), 159.

4. I use the form 'Astrophil' throughout my text, with the support of Ringler, p. 458, of Kenneth Muir in a review of Ringler, *R.N.* xvi (1963), 231, and of Mona Wilson, ed., *Astrophel and Stella*, 1931, pp. xvi–xvii. I am not impressed by the argument of Michel Poirier, in *E.A.* xvii (1964), 70, that the form 'Astrophel' may have been preferred by Sidney or by his early editors because it 'unit par l'homophonie les noms des deux amoureux', and I can find no warrant for Fred Inglis's assertion in *The Elizabethan Poets: The Making of English Poetry from Wyatt to Ben Jonson*, 1969, p. 74, that 'Astrophel' means 'stargazer'. 'Astrophil' means 'star-lover', and so implies 'lover of Stella', and has the further advantage of including the first syllable of Sidney's Christian name: he delighted in this sort of ingenuity.

5. Muir, *Sir Philip Sidney*, 1967, p. 30.

6. Young, p. 41, contrasts it with Sonnets 3 and 6.

7. Ibid., p. 11.   8. Rudenstine, p. 193.   9. Ringler, p. 168.

to various gods for qualities which they notoriously do not possess:

> Like great god *Saturn* faire, and like faire *Venus* chaste:
> As smooth as *Pan*, as *Juno* milde, like goddesse *Isis* faste.
> With *Cupid* she fore-sees, and goes god *Vulcan's* pace:
> And for a tast of all these gifts, she borowes *Momus'* grace.[1]

This is very obvious dispraise. Sonnet 9 is much more like Sonnets 3 and 6 of *Astrophil and Stella*,[2] in which various elaborate and conventional ways of praising Stella are rejected and yet at the same time used to build the poems. In Sonnet 9 the conventional imagery is intended more seriously, it is true, but Astrophil winks occasionally at the reader to show that he is quite aware of what he is doing and of how ridiculous it may at times appear.

There is half a wink at the word 'now' (with the implication: 'the next stage in these proceedings is . . .') at the beginning of the sestet:

> The windowes now through which this heav'nly guest
> Looks over the world, and can find nothing such,
> Which dare claime from those lights the name of best,
> Of touch they are . . .

And this leads to the sudden intrusion of Cupid, deliberately shocking in a poem which has been praising Stella for her spiritual qualities,[3] and a complicated set of puns on the word 'touch' which is all the more striking after the comparative simplicity and formality of the poem's octave:

> Of touch they are that without touch doth touch,
> Which *Cupid's* selfe from Beautie's myne did draw:
> Of touch they are, and poore I am their straw.

It is not surprising that these lines have been so often discussed,[4] for they contain a wealth of meaning. First, Stella's eyes are said to

---

1. *O.A.* 3, ibid., p. 12.　　2. Ibid., pp. 166, 167.
3. D. L. Peterson, *The English Lyric from Wyatt to Donne*, 1967, p. 189. See also Rudenstine, p. 239, on 'disrupted praise'.
4. S. A. Cowan and F. A. Dudley, 'Sidney's *Astrophel and Stella*, IX', *Explicator*, xx, no. 9 (1961–2), Article 76; Lever, p. 77; Peterson, loc. cit.; Michel Poirier ed. and trans., *Sir Philip Sidney: Astrophel and Stella*, 1957, pp. 196–7; Max Putzel, 'Sidney's *Astrophel and Stella*, IX', *Explicator*, xix, no. 4 (1960–1), Article 25; Ringler, pp. 463–4; Mona Wilson, ed., *Astrophel and Stella*, p. 162. In my discussion I draw upon all these.

be 'of touch', that is, like glossy black marble used for expensive tombs and buildings (her eyes are beautiful and precious) and like basanite used to test the quality of gold or silver alloys. 'Without touch' means without physical contact, and at the same time reminds us that there is such a thing as physical contact although the poem has ignored this previously. 'Doth touch' has two senses: affects emotionally, and tests the worth of (here the worth of Stella's lover). That the touch has been drawn by Cupid from 'Beautie's myne' continues, of course, the senses of black marble and basanite, but it also suggests explosive (mine in the sense of a tunnel dug under the walls of a besieged town, as in Sonnet 2 of *Astrophil and Stella*).[5] 'Of touch they are' has the sense of a black stone again (jet this time) which, when magnetized by rubbing, has the power of drawing light bodies to itself, and also the sense of touchwood, or tinder, to burn the straw. I think Sidney intends both meanings here: Astrophil is first drawn to the eyes and then burnt up in them. Finally, behind all these meanings of 'touch' runs the suggestion of physical contact, which is in sharp contrast to the previous praise of Stella for her spiritual qualities.

It is small wonder that Sidney has been credited with 'the modern grace of ambiguity'.[6] And this is not merely a display of virtuosity;[7] meanings are multiplied, not for the sake of it, but to convey the complexity of Astrophil's feelings. Astrophil is both perplexed and, at the same time, remarkably lucid in expressing his perplexity. George Gascoigne would have approved:

. . . it is not inough to roll in pleasant woordes, nor yet to thunder in *Rym, Ram, Ruff,* by letter (quoth my master *Chaucer*) nor yet to abounde in apt vocables, or epythetes, unlesse the Invention have in it also *aliquid salis.* By this *aliquid salis,* I meane some good and fine devise, shewing the quicke capacitie of a writer . . .[8]

Ingenuity, wit, and humour pervade Sidney's work. His *Apology for Poetry,* for instance, owes its success not only to its shrewd and lucid arguments but also, and perhaps even more, to

5. Ringler, p. 165.
6. Anon., 'High Erected Thoughts' (review of *inter alia* Craik, op. cit.), *T.L.S.,* 6 January 1966, p. 5.
7. As suggested by Montgomery, p. 80.
8. 'Certayne notes of Instruction *concerning the making of verse or ryme* in English, written at the request of Master *Edouardo Donati', The Complete Works of George Gascoigne,* ed. J. W. Cunliffe, 1907, i, 465. Gascoigne's essay was first published in 1575; see John Buxton, *A Tradition of English Poetry,* 1967, p. 44.

its easy, familiar manner and frequent touches of humour.[9] There
is the lordly but loving scorn with which Sidney dismisses all
possible challengers of poetry's right to be considered as 'the
highest point of man's wit':[1] 'the astronomer looking to the stars
might fall into a ditch',[2] we are told, and moral philosophers are
pictured 'sophistically speaking against subtlety, and angry with
any man in whom they see the foul fault of anger'.[3] Not, I hope, to
labour the point, we may see how, at the end of the following
extract, Sidney jokes the reader into preferring fiction to fact, or at
least, charms him into a mood in which he will be more receptive
of arguments in favour of fiction:

. . . let us take one example wherein a poet and a historian do concur.
Herodotus and Justin do both testify that Zopyrus, King Darius'
faithful servant, seeing his master long resisted by the rebellious
Babylonians, feigned himself in extreme disgrace of his king: for
verifying of which, he caused his own nose and ears to be cut off, and so
flying to the Babylonians, was received, and for his known valour so
far credited, that he did find means to deliver them over to Darius.
Much like matter doth Livy record of Tarquinius and his son. Xenophon
excellently feigneth such another stratagem performed by Abradatas in
Cyrus' behalf. Now would I fain know, if occasion be presented unto
you to serve your prince by such an honest dissimulation, why you do
not as well learn it of Xenophon's fiction as of the other's verity? And
truly so much the better, as you shall save your nose by the bargain;
for Abradatas did not counterfeit so far.[4]

However doubtful a reader may be of the morality of the *real-
politik* which Sidney approves of here, and however aware that a
joke is not necessarily an argument, he can hardly fail to be tickled.
But the humour is not always so obvious; it comes often in unlikely places, and may easily be missed by a rapid or over-solemn
reader. The critic who, after praising the *Apology* for its urbanity,[5]
bewails a falling-off in the style of the peroration, which he
regards simply as 'an argument addressed to the personal ambition
of the reader',[6] has missed the tone of friendly mockery:

. . . believe themselves [i.e., poets], when they tell you they will make
you immortal by their verses.

9. F. S. Boas, *Sir Philip Sidney, Representative Elizabethan: His Life and Writings*,
1955, p. 56; Kenneth Muir, *Sir Philip Sidney*, p. 10; K. O. Myrick, *Sir Philip Sidney
as a Literary Craftsman*, 1935, p. 78.

1. Shepherd, p. 101.   2. Ibid., p. 104.   3. Ibid., p. 105.
4. Ibid., pp. 110–11.   5. Symonds, op. cit., p. 157.   6. Ibid., p. 168.

Thus doing, your name shall flourish in the printers' shops; thus doing, you shall be of kin to many a poetical preface; thus doing, you shall be most fair, most rich, most wise, most all; you shall dwell upon superlatives.[7]

A question worth asking is why Sidney, who planned his *Apology* very carefully,[8] should choose to end it in such a flippant manner. Even more interesting, why should he speak so flippantly of his own poetry?

. . . I will give you a nearer example of myself, who (I know not by what mischance) in these my not old years and idlest times having slipped into the title of a poet, am provoked to say something unto you in the defence of that my unelected vocation . . .[9]

This is sound tactics at the opening of the *Apology*, of course: Sidney charms the reader by his modesty at the same time that he gives a gentle reminder that this defender of poetry is someone who knows about it from the inside; he is not only a theoretician. Yet Sidney habitually speaks of his own literary works in a studiously offhand manner.[1] It is a neat way of disarming criticism, and Sidney's close friend Sir Fulke Greville admits using it as a recognized rhetorical device with that intention, describing it as 'that hypocriticall figure *Ironia*, wherein men commonly (to keep above their workes) seeme to make toies of the utmost they can doe'.[2] In Sidney, however, the device is used so often as to reveal a fairly consistent attitude or cast of mind.

It would be a great mistake to presume that Sidney wanted to be taken literally, that he did not regard his works as important.[3] He was, rather, adopting the manner then considered appropriate to the ideal courtier, the manner advocated in Castiglione's influential work which had been translated into English when Sidney was a child.[4] Count Lodovico da Canossa says that the courtier should

use in every thyng a certain Reckelesness, to cover art withall, and seeme whatsoever he doth and sayeth to do it wythout pain, and (as it were)

7. Shepherd, p. 142.   8. Ibid., pp. 11–17; Myrick, op. cit., pp. 46–83.
9. Shepherd, p. 95.
1. e.g., dedication to *The Countesse of Pembrokes Arcadia* in *The Complete Works of Sir Philip Sidney*, ed. Albert Feuillerat, 1939, i, 3–4.
2. *Sir Fulke Greville's Life of Sir Philip Sidney* (1652), ed. Nowell Smith, 1907, p. 154.
3. Muir, *Sir Philip Sidney*, p. 5; Myrick, op. cit., pp. 3–45.
4. W. G. Crane, *Wit and Rhetoric in the Renaissance: The Formal Basis of Elizabethan Prose Style*, 1964, p. 127: 'Castiglione's *Il libro del cortegiano*, 1528, which Sir Thomas Hoby translated into English in 1561, was by far the most important book on courtly conduct of the sixteenth century.'

not myndyng it. And of thys do I beleve grace is muche deryved, for in rare matters and wel brought to passe every man knoweth the hardnes of them, so that a rediness therin maketh great wonder. And contrary-wise to use force, and (as they say) to hale by the hear, geveth a great disgrace, and maketh every thing how great so ever it be, to be little estemed. Therfore that may be said to be a very art that appeereth not to be art . . .[5]

A modern translator uses, for Hoby's 'Reckelesness', the word 'nonchalance',[6] and sometimes in English the Italian term 'sprez-zatura' is used. Whatever we care to call it, when the quality is defined in the *Book of the Courtier* it has already been displayed by Unico Aretino. He seems very anxious to discover the meaning of the letter 'S' which the Duchess of Urbino is wearing on her fore-head. He is so anxious to know that he suggests that everyone present should say what he believes the meaning to be. There are no takers and so, as luck will have it, Aretino himself is asked to supply a meaning. He has to be asked more than once:

Unico, after he had pawsed a while being stil called upon to say his fansy, at length rehersed a rime upon the aforesaide matter, expound-ynge what signified the letter S, the which many judged to be made at the first sight. But bicause it was more witty and better knitt then a man would have beleved the shortnes of time required, it was thought he had prepared it before.[7]

We wholly mistake the nature of this ideal if we imagine that it was only trivial actions which had to be performed with studied insouciance. It may well be that the ideal cost Sidney his life. Before the battle of Zutphen, when he had already put on his cuisses, he took them off again when he saw the Lord Marshal was not wearing his;[8] and it was in one of his unarmoured thighs that he received the fatal wound. We do not know why the Lord Mar-shal was inadequately clothed (he may have been merely forgetful), but Sidney's action was deliberate and seems to have come from the desire not to appear too serious or concerned about the coming battle.

It was an aristocratic ideal, part and parcel in those days of being a gifted amateur. When I say that Sidney was an amateur poet, I do

5. Baldesar Castiglione, *The Book of the Courtier*, trans. Sir Thomas Hoby (1561), ed. W. E. Henley, 1900, p. 59.
6. George Bull, *The Book of the Courtier*, 1967, p. 67.
7. Castiglione, op. cit., p. 39.   8. Muir, *Sir Philip Sidney*, p. 7.

not mean that his poems were not made with the highest standards in mind. I mean that they were the products of someone with the leisure to write and the obligation—whatever his financial position—never to expect any money for them.[9] It is difficult for us now to imagine a cast of mind which regarded venturing into print as vulgar, something done only by *hoi polloi* like Spenser, Drayton, and Ben Jonson: nowadays we reserve such finer feelings for sport. Nevertheless, the feeling was strong in Sidney's set, and it persisted long after his day.

Sidney's social position raised him above the need for patronage[1] and gave his poetry a certain lordly air which might seem offensive to us now if it were not for the pervasive Sidneyan charm. In some ways he is remarkable for what he did *not* write about. It is surprising to find an Elizabethan poet leaving behind him thousands of lines of verse and yet devoting only twelve of them to praise of the Queen.[2] This may show only a lack of personal interest in the subject, and it is true that another famous amateur poet, Sir Walter Ralegh (who seems to have disdained print as much as Sidney),[3] wrote a number of poems in praise of Elizabeth.[4] However, Ralegh did have one or two blunders to redeem,[5] and anyway he was not quite out of the top drawer: I think Sidney's high social position may well account for his apparent failure to recognize the Queen's superlative worth. It is also noticeable, and has several times been remarked upon,[6] that Astrophil nowhere promises to make Stella immortal by his verse, although the promise of immortality is made again and again by those who followed Sidney in the sonnet tradition.[7] Maybe this just happens to be one sonnet convention which Sidney forgot to propagate; but it is probably significant that Daniel, Drayton, and

9. E. H. Miller, *The Professional Writer in Elizabethan England: A Study of Nondramatic Literature*, 1959, pp. 6–7, 22, 151.

1. J. F. Danby, *Elizabethan and Jacobean Poets*, 1965, pp. 31, 33.

2. The poem is in Ringler, p. 3.

3. Agnes Latham, ed., *The Poems of Sir Walter Ralegh*, 1962, p. xxiv.

4. e.g., ibid., pp. 24, 25–44.   5. Ibid., pp. xvi, xxxvii.

6. L. C. John, *The Elizabethan Sonnet Sequences: Studies in Conventional Conceits*, 1938, p. 130; Poirier, *Sir Philip Sidney: Astrophel and Stella*, p. 26; Poirier, *Sir Philip Sidney, Le Chevalier Poète Élizabéthain*, 1948, p. 302; Mona Wilson, ed., *Astrophel and Stella*, p. xvi.

7. e.g., Samuel Daniel, *Delia*, Sonnets XXX, XXXIIII, *Poems and A Defence of Ryme*, ed. A. C. Sprague, 1950, pp. 25, 27; Michael Drayton, *Idea*, Sonnets 5, 22, *Poems of Michael Drayton*, ed. John Buxton, 1953, i, 5, 13; William Shakespeare, *Sonnets* 15, 18, 19, ed. J. Dover Wilson, 1966, pp. 10–12.

Shakespeare were writing for patrons—peers perhaps, but not equals.

The age of specialization was already coming in Sidney's life-time, and the great achievements in drama so soon after his death were the work of professionals; but Sidney stands for a different way of life. To him writing is an important pursuit indeed, neces-sary to complete the courtly gentleman's all-round perfection,[8] but still only one of the many skills required by the Magnanimous Man. This all-round perfection is what Spenser calls magnificence and, for his *Faerie Queene*, embodies in the person of Prince Arthur:

> . . . *in the person of Prince Arthure I sette forth magnificence in particular, which vertue for that (according to Aristotle and the rest) it is the perfection of all the rest, and conteineth in it them all, therefore in the whole course I mention the deedes of Arthure applyable to that vertue, which I write of in that booke.*[9]

There is little humility in this notion,[1] and it must be insisted that Sidney's nonchalance about his literary works is very far from being evidence of humility; it is a means by which a writer may keep himself above his works.[2]

To us it may seem ridiculous that a man of such obvious literary talent should throw his life away in a battle;[3] but in the Renais-sance it was a commonplace that virtue was essentially an active quality,[4] and that therefore action was more important than writ-ing. Even the dedicated professional Ben Jonson admits (rather grudgingly perhaps, but still admits) the superiority of action:

> Although to write be lesser then to doo,
> It is the next deed, and a great one too.[5]

Again, more than half a century after Sidney's death Milton, who from his early years had been preparing himself for the production of a great literary work, chose to spend the prime of his life in politics and pamphleteering.

It is part of Sidney's fascination that, even when he is writing,

---

8. Danby, op. cit., p. 32.
9. 'A Letter of the Author's to Sir Walter Raleigh', Spenser, p. 407.
1. C. S. Lewis, *English Literature in the Sixteenth Century, Excluding Drama* (vol. iii of *The Oxford History of English Literature*), 1962, p. 53.
2. See the quotation from Greville, p. 8 above.
3. Sidney Lee, *Great Englishmen of the Sixteenth Century*, 1907, p. 42.
4. G. K. Hunter, 'Humanism and Courtship', *Elizabethan Poetry: Modern Essays in Criticism*, ed. P. J. Alpers, 1967, p. 8.
5. *Ben Jonson*, ed. C. H. Herford, Percy and Evelyn Simpson, 1947, viii, 61.

he never seems to be only a writer[6]—the sense of a wide world outside the limits of a sonnet is often very strong. Astrophil may be indifferent to current political problems, but Sidney knows all about them:

> Whether the Turkish new-moone minded be
>   To fill his hornes this yeare on Christian coast;
>   How *Poles'* right king meanes, without leave of hoast,
> To warme with ill-made fire cold *Moscovy*;
> If French can yet three parts in one agree . . .
> These questions busie wits to me do frame;
>   I, cumbred with good maners, answer do,
>   But know not how, for still I thinke of you.[7]

A poem may be composed on horseback, in the intervals of a busy life:

> Highway since you my chiefe *Pernassus* be,
>   And that my Muse to some eares not unsweet,
>   Tempers her words to trampling horses feet,
> More oft then to a chamber melodie;
> Now blessed you, beare onward blessed me . . .[8]

Perhaps it was not composed on horseback—we must always beware of taking any poet too literally—but it is still significant that Astrophil said it was.

Perhaps the best epitaph on Sidney is that made by Sir Walter Ralegh in which the many-sidedness of the hero is emphasized, and yet not merely his many-sidedness but also his perfection in every pursuit:

> That day their Haniball died, our Scipio fell,
> Scipio, Cicero, and Petrarch of our time,
> Whose vertues wounded by my woorthles rime,
> Let Angels speake, and heauens thy praises tell.[9]

6. Jean Robertson, 'Sir Philip Sidney and his Poetry', *Elizabethan Poetry* (Stratford-upon-Avon Studies 2), general editors J. R. Brown and Bernard Harris, 1960, p. 111.

7. *A.S.* 30, Ringler, pp. 179–80.

8. *A.S.* 84, ibid., p. 209. I take it that Astrophil means in line 1 simply that he often composed while travelling, despite this suggested paraphrase: 'You are my way to poetry because you lead me to Stella', ibid., p. 483.

9. Latham, ed. cit., p. 7. A footnote in this edition mentions that the Spanish commander, Hannibal Gonzago, also died of wounds at Zutphen: Ralegh's use of this fact is a neat example of *aliquid salis*, which Gascoigne required in poetry (p. 6 above).

The aristocrat must not only do everything, but do everything very well: even the expression of grief must have an air of distinction about it:

> Sorrow onely then hath glory,
> When tis excellently sory.[1]

Unfortunately, there are some things which even an aristocrat might be well advised to steer clear of. There is reason to believe that Sidney regarded the ancient sort of versifying which 'marked the quantity of each syllable, and according to that framed his verse'[2] as particularly suitable to the high-born.[3] He also believed that quantitative verse was 'more fit for music',[4] and it is true that all the poems in the *Old Arcadia* which are meant to be in quantity are described as being sung, not simply recited.[5] How they sounded when sung, however, no one knows.[6] Now, it is not impossible to write English verse in which long and short syllables are arranged in patterns; but to attempt to do so while regarding length of syllable as a stronger structural principle than stress is to ask for trouble. However, *noblesse oblige*, and Sidney tried it. He was even careful to draw attention to his experiments by providing notations of the metres he was using.[7]

It is difficult now even to sympathize with the effort,[8] and, if it is rather unfair to deny all poetical value to Sidney's experiments in this manner,[9] such value as they sometimes have does seem to be an accidental one. There can be poetry in these verses, but it occurs in spite of their being written in quantity, or rather their being written in what was *meant* to be quantity.

Of course, Sidney was not the first to make the attempt.[1] Ascham, for instance, had been against rhyming[2] (usually opposed to quantity,[3] although they do not have to be mutually exclusive)

1. *A.S. Ninth song*, Ringler, p. 221.   2. Shepherd, p. 140.
3. Ringler, p. 393.
4. Shepherd, p. 140. See also Buxton, *Sir Philip Sidney and the English Renaissance*, 1954, p. 116.
5. Ringler, pp. 392–3.   6. Ibid., p. 393.
7. James Applegate, 'Sidney's Classical Metres', *M.L.N.* lxx (1955), 255.
8. There is a good attempt to make us sympathize in B. M. Hollowell, 'The Elizabethan Hexametrists', *P.Q.* iii (1924), 51–7.
9. As does Symonds, op. cit., p. 92.
1. For a brief account of early experiments see Ringler, p. 390.
2. Roger Ascham, 'Of Imitation' (from *The Scholemaster*, 1570), *Elizabethan Critical Essays*, ed. G. Gregory Smith, 1904, i, 29–31.
3. As by Sidney himself in Shepherd, p. 140.

and in favour of verse which observed 'trew quantitie in euery foote and sillable, as onelie the learned shalbe able to do, and as the *Grekes* and *Romanes* were wont to do . . .'.[4] There had for a long time been considerable confusion as to what was the fundamental principle of English verse, even among those who could and did write good accentual verse.[5] Writers seem to have sensed the importance of stress to English metre, without being able to think out their intuitions fully.[6] Whatever they were trying to do when they wrote in quantity (and there is real doubt what it was they were trying to do),[7] they were always forced when writing English verse to take some account of stress: the language demanded it.[8]

Sidney's own rules for the writing of quantitative verse in English have been preserved.[9] Briefly, these are the same as for Latin verse: some syllables are naturally short, some are naturally long, and short vowels generally become long when followed by more than one consonant. The strangest rule is that of length by position: the length of a vowel in English is simply not affected by the number of consonants which follow it. Moreover, given the confused state of spelling in Sidney's day, it was possible to make any syllable theoretically long simply by altering the spelling; this made the rules fairly easy to keep, without making them worth keeping. It was this orthographical juggling which exposed how factitious and pointless the whole exercise was.[1] Adding an extra letter or two does of course make a syllable occupy more space on the page, but it is hard to imagine that this was all that was intended: we are led to infer a belief that spelling could actually affect pronunciation, that it was possible to make a syllable sound longer. It was known that Greek quantitative measures had been deliberately adapted to Latin verse,[2] and it was believed apparently that the same thing could be done in English. Whereas we tend to think of a poet accommodating the kind of verse he writes to the nature of the language, the nature of the language being something already settled, Sidney and some of his contemporaries

4. Ascham, op. cit., 31.
5. J. B. Broadbent, *Poetic Love*, 1964, p. 65; G. D. Willcock, 'Passing Pitefull Hexameters: A Study of Quantity and Accent in English Renaissance Verse', *M.L.R.* xxix (1934), 1–3.
6. Willcock, op. cit., 4.
7. John Thompson, *The Founding of English Metre*, 1961, p. 135.   8. Ibid.
9. Printed and discussed in Ringler, pp. 391–2.
1. Robertson, op. cit., p. 123; Willcock, op. cit., p. 5.
2. John Hollander, 'The Music of Poetry', *J.A.A.C.* xv (1956), 235.

seem to have thought it possible to alter the nature of the language radically by a conscious effort.[3] They could not succeed; but the attempt itself is a striking indication of the importance they attached to conscious contrivance in the writing of poetry.

The results can be intriguing. For instance, we come across a line in perfect stressed hendecasyllabics: 'What man grafts in a tree dissimulation?'[4] but we come across it in a poem ostensibly written in quantity in the First Asclepiadean metre! Turning to a poem intended to be in quantitative hendecasyllabics, we find that the most successful lines are those which have a pattern of stresses as well as of 'quantity':

> *Reason, tell me thy mind, if here be reason*
> In this strange violence, to make resistance.
> *Where sweet graces erect the stately banner*
> Of vertue's regiment, shining in harnesse
> Of fortune's Diademes, by beauty mustred.
> *Say then Reason, I say what is thy counsell?*[5]

In another poem also we find that success (that is, a recognizable, audible pattern to the verse) has come where stress and quantity coincide:

> My muse what ails this ardour
> To blase my onely secretts?
> Alas it is no glory
> To sing my owne decaid state.[6]

Thus Sidney occasionally hit by accident (and without, so far as we know, realizing it) on what seems the obvious way to accommodate classical metres to English—an accentual imitation of the classical metrical patterns.[7] This was what was done later by Campion: he used as long syllables only those obviously long (avoiding the many in English whose length is dubious), he did not make length dependent on position, and he chose words in which stress and quantity coincided.[8] This solution has the difficulty that it seriously limits the number of words which a poet can use,[9] but it does give metrical lines.

---

3. Willcock, op. cit., pp. 9–10.
4. Ringler, p. 69. We need to read 'dissimulation' as five syllables, which was allowable in Sidney's day.
5. Ibid., p. 67. I have italicized the relevant lines.
6. Ibid., p. 65.   7. Willcock, op. cit., p. 6.   8. Robertson, op. cit., p. 124.
9. Ibid.; Willcock, op. cit., p. 16.

The next step would be to forget about quantity (at least as a regular structural element) and simply imitate the classical metrical patterns, using stress. In German, a language in which stress is as important as it is in English, this has been done frequently and successfully for hundreds of years. Tennyson did it:

> O you chorus of indolent reviewers,
> Irresponsible, indolent reviewers,
> Look, I come to the test, a tiny poem
> All composed in a metre of Catullus,
> All in quantity, careful of my motion . . .[1]

Tennyson seems to have known what he was doing, since he said that his lines 'must be read with the English accent',[2] but even with him a confusion of terms is noticeable: he says in the poem itself that he is writing 'All in quantity' when that very line has a syllable ('of'), which, preserving the stress pattern admirably, certainly is not long. This is far from being the only example in the poem of a short syllable taking a stress. Again, one wonders whether the irregularity of another line is not caused by some memory of the classical rule of length by position:

> O blatant Magazines, regard me rather . . .[3]

The second syllable of 'blatant' would be long by the classical rules, but it does not take a stress, and it should.

Such examples as this, and others of Tennyson,[4] suggest that the story is not ended yet: there is still scope for fruitful experiment.[5] Nevertheless, Sidney's achievements in this line are not very striking. Perhaps his experiments in quantity had the value of making him think harder about the nature of English words, and perhaps they helped eventually to improve his accentual lines;[6] and perhaps they did neither.

The imitation of classical metres was a minority pursuit: some other forms of imitation were not. In plundering previous writers for themes, phrases, and images Sidney was like any other poet of

---

1. *The Poems of Tennyson*, ed. Christopher Ricks, 1969, p. 1155.
2. Ibid.   3. Ibid., p. 1156.   4. Ibid., pp. 1154–5.
5. Two recent examples of the accentual use of classical patterns, both fine poems and not interesting merely as experiments, are W. H. Auden's 'Down There' (in scazons) and 'Up There' (in hendecasyllabics), *About the House*, 1966, pp. 24–5.
6. Theodore Spencer, 'The Poetry of Sir Philip Sidney', *E.L.H.* xii (1945), 257–9.

his time, learned or unlearned, courtly or uncourtly. He was in fact doing what all poets, in any age, do; that it was done in his day more systematically, consciously, and—above all—without a guilty conscience is what makes it a matter worth discussing.

I presume that there is no longer any need to spend space rebutting the notion that, if we can find sources for a poem, then that poem is in some way 'insincere' or 'unoriginal'.[7] Sidney Lee's attitude, involving the use of terms like 'plagiarism'[8] and 'literary pirates'[9] and the grudging admission that 'wholesale loans . . . did not always succeed in extinguishing the buoyant native fire',[1] is by now merely a historical curiosity.

Our knowledge of Sidney's indebtedness to other poets has grown considerably since Lee's day,[2] and so has our understanding of it. For instance, it is now clear that a writer of love poems in the Renaissance was not so much a solitary expressing powerful private emotions as a man doing exactly what was expected of him and what others had done before him; his borrowings show his awareness that he is joining an honourable company.[3] The writing of poetry was a public action, and the writer would naturally show he knew what had been done before and, in his own achievement, make plain the personal variations he had worked on time-honoured themes.[4]

Ascham's discussion of imitation,[5] published when Sidney was a youth, is worth some mention since it sums up much of what was taken for granted in Elizabethan England. Ascham points out that all languages are learned solely by imitation.[6] We may expand what he says to stress that a child can only learn to speak by imitating (to some extent, parrot-fashion) the language he hears about him. Thus, at the very beginning of our lives we use, in using language, something that is not our own: we are performing a conventional action and using conventional means. The poet, we may add, the poet of any period, is doing something similar even though he is doing it in a more sophisticated manner.

---

7. Patricia Thomson, review of Kalstone, *M.L.R.* lxi (1966), 487.
8. 'The Elizabethan Sonnet', *The Cambridge History of English Literature*, ed. A. W. Ward and A. R. Waller, 1909, iii, 248.
9. *Elizabethan Sonnets, Newly Arranged and Indexed*, 1904, I, xxxiv.
1. Ibid.   2. Lever, pp. 54–5.   3. Ibid., p. 56.
4. Lever, pp. 58–62, brings this out very well by a comparison of *A.S.* 71 with its source in Petrarch.
5. Ascham, op. cit.   6. Ibid., 5.

Ascham recommends to the vernacular writer that he study the Greeks and Romans as 'the trewe Paterne of Eloquence'.[7] This idea of the superiority of the classics was a very powerful one and survived long after Ascham's time, but with Sidney and many others it did not exclude the possibility of imitating other writers —the Italians, the French, in fact anyone and anything from which something might be learned. What is most important in Ascham's recommendation is the implication that a writer must learn his art and ought to know which are the best teachers.

Ascham even gives a warning still relevant to the modern source-hunter. Merely to indicate borrowings[8] is, he says, 'but a colde helpe to the encrease of learning'.[9] He tells us what we should do:

But if a man would take his paine also, whan he hath layd two places of *Homer* and *Virgill* or of *Demosthenes* and *Tullie* togither, to teach plainlie withall, after this sort:

1. *Tullie* reteyneth thus moch of the matter, thies sentences, thies wordes:

2. This and that he leaueth out, which he doth wittelie to this end and purpose.

3. This he addeth here.

4. This he diminisheth there.

5. This he ordereth thus, with placing that here, not there.

6. This he altereth and changeth, either in propertie of wordes, in forme of sentence, in substance of the matter, or in one or other conuenient circumstance of the authors present purpose.

In thies fewe rude English wordes are wrapt vp all the necessarie tooles and instrumentes, where with trewe *Imitation* is rightlie wrought withall in any tongue.[1]

Here again there is an interesting implication. Our awareness of a writer's indebtedness to other writers, far from lessening in our eyes the value of his work, should increase our understanding of his peculiar contribution to the tradition. We may find, for instance, that he makes more far-reaching adaptations of his sources in his mature work than in his apprentice work.[2]

7. Ascham, op. cit., 22.

8. As is done by A. M. Lyles, 'A Note on Sidney's Use of Chaucer', *N.Q.* cxcviii (1953), 99–100; J. H. Walter, '*Astrophel and Stella* and *The Romaunt of the Rose*', *R.E.S.* xv (1939), 265–73.

9. Ascham, op. cit., 9.   1. Ibid. See also note 4, p. 17, above.

2. Poirier, 'Quelques Sources des Poèmes de Sidney', *E.A.* xi (1958), 150–4.

No one could be more scathing than Sidney on the subject of indiscriminate and unimaginative borrowing:

Truly I could wish, if at least I might be so bold to wish in a thing beyond the reach of my capacity, the diligent imitators of Tully and Demosthenes (most worthy to be imitated) did not so much keep Nizolian paper-books of their figures and phrases, as by attentive translation (as it were) devour them whole, and make them wholly theirs.[3]

It is not a sparse diet of other writers which Sidney recommends here, but simply a good digestion. Hardin Craig takes up Sidney's metaphor of eating in his witty summary of the outlook of Renaissance writers:

. . . their theory—and it is surprising how successfully it worked in their hands—was one which made them, on the authority of Quintilian and the great Italians, believe in absorbing into themselves the merits of the greatest and best writers of antiquity and the modern world in somewhat the same way as a cannibal chief might increase his own prowess by devouring his worthier enemies.[4]

Sidney's comments on imitation in *Astrophil and Stella* require a sophisticated response from the reader:

> Let daintie wits crie on the Sisters nine,
> That bravely maskt, their fancies may be told:
> Or *Pindare's* Apes, flaunt they in phrases fine,
> Enam'ling with pied flowers their thoughts of gold . . .[5]

For eight lines Sidney lists material used in poetry, and then says he will not use it because he cannot:

> Phrases and Problemes from my reach do grow,
> And strange things cost too deare for my poore sprites.

The point is, of course, that he has, in the very act of rejecting it, made use of this material for this poem and demonstrated that his 'sprites' are far from 'poore'. To disclaim artistry and ingenuity in the act of using them is a stroke of artistry and ingenuity in itself. It involves humour too, the same kind of humour that we have

---

3. Shepherd, p. 138.
4. *The Enchanted Glass: The Elizabethan Mind in Literature*, 1936, p. 254.
5. Sonnet 3, Ringler, p. 166. P. N. Siegel, 'A Suggested Emendation for one of Sidney's Sonnets', *N.Q.* cxciv (1949), 75–6, suggests that '*Pindare's* Apes' should be emended to 'Petrarch's apes'; but see the note on this line in Ringler, p. 460.

when indebtedness to other writers is denied in words that themselves constitute a debt:[6]

> I never dranke of *Aganippe* well,
> Nor ever did in shade of *Tempe* sit:
> And Muses scorne with vulgar braines to dwell,
> Poore Layman I, for sacred rites unfit.
>   Some do I heare of Poets' furie tell,
> But (God wot) wot not what they meane by it:
> And this I sweare by blackest brooke of hell,
> I am no pick-purse of another's wit.[7]

In the third sonnet the denial of reliance on any other material
than '*Stella's* face' makes a fine compliment for her, a compliment
that is made more subtle and civilized and not destroyed by the
fact that the end of the poem is patently untrue:

> . . . in *Stella's* face I reed,
> What Love and Beautie be, then all my deed
> But Copying is, what in her Nature writes.[8]

Sidney is fond of mocking imitation; but it must be insisted
that mockery is itself a use of the thing mocked. We may laugh at
lovers

> Who thinke themselves well blest, if they renew
> Some good old dumpe, that *Chaucer's* mistresse knew,[9]

but they are brought to mind by these lines, and we enjoy the
recollection. Mockery of a tradition then becomes one way of
using it without being subservient to it: the cannibal chief gains
strength from his enemies by eating them, not by worshipping
them.

Sidney's best-known poem on this subject, 'You that do search
for everie purling spring',[1] is, not unexpectedly, a good-humoured
attack on the unimaginative use of tradition.[2] Poets 'take wrong
waies' when they 'search for *everie* purling spring', and 'wring'
'*everie* floure, *not sweet perhaps*'[3] into their poetry. They lack the
'inward tuch' necessary to make proper use of what is stolen.

---

6. Muir, *Sir Philip Sidney*, pp. 28–9.   7. Sonnet 74, Ringler, pp. 203–4.
8. Ibid., p. 166.   9. *C.S.* 17, ibid., p. 146.
1. *A.S.* 15, ibid., p. 172.   2. Montgomery, p. 70.
3. My italics.

Whether he is mocking it or not, the poet who can use a tradition intelligently and show that he is doing so gains support from it. The sonnet 'Leave me ô Love, which reachest but to dust'[4] reminds me in one way of Milton's sonnets: deliberate echoes of the Bible and the Book of Common Prayer imply that Sidney is not merely expressing a personal point of view; his lines are given a greater authority by being shown to be part of the time-honoured Christian tradition:[5]

> Leave me ô Love, which reachest but to dust,
> And thou my mind aspire to higher things:
> Grow rich in that which never taketh rust:
> What ever fades, but fading pleasure brings.

The imagery of the third line is obviously meant to bring to mind the famous passage from Matthew's Gospel on the Kingdom of Heaven:

Lay not vp treasures for your selues vpon the earth, where the moth and canker corrupt . . . But lay vp treasures for your selues in heauen, where neither the moth nor canker corrupteth . . . For where your treasure is, there will your heart be also.[6]

In the second quatrain the mention of 'that sweet yoke, where lasting freedomes be' is an echo of a prayer to God 'in knowledge of whom standeth our eternal life, whose service is perfect freedom';[7] also

> the light,
> That doth both shine and give us sight to see

echoes a Psalm:

> . . . in thy light shall we see light.[8]

4. *C.S.* 32, Ringler, p. 161.
5. For Milton see, e.g., 'Avenge O Lord thy slaughter'd Saints' and 'When I consider how my light is spent', *Milton's Sonnets*, ed. E. A. J. Honigmann, 1966, and the commentaries on pp. 162–8 and 169–76.
6. Matt. 6. 19–21, Geneva Version. Verse 19 is quoted in *O.E.D.* (canker sb. 2) to illustrate the use of 'canker' with the meaning of 'rust'; the date of the first instance of this usage quoted is 1533. That Sidney echoes these verses is noted by Craik, op. cit., p. 244.
7. The Book of Common Prayer, the second collect at Morning Prayer. The echo is noted by Craik, op. cit., p. 244.
8. Psalm 36. 9, Geneva Version.

Then,

>   thinke how evill becommeth him to slide,
>   Who seeketh heav'n, and comes of heav'nly breath

echoes, more faintly it is true:

The Lord God also made the man of the dust of the groūd, & breathed in his face breath of life, & the man was a liuing soule.[9]

Finally, the common echo helps us to connect these lines with the first line of the poem:

>   Leave me ô Love, which reachest but to dust,

and to see more clearly the contrast between two kinds of love which is the theme of the poem.

This contrast is emphasized also by using the word 'Love' in the first line and in the last line while qualifying it differently on each occasion. In the first line it is the love 'which reachest but to dust', but in the last line it is 'Eternall Love'. This is a reminder of how carefully and apparently consciously constructed Sidney's poems are. Again, in the line 'What ever fades, but fading pleasure brings' the repetition, with a difference, in 'fades' and 'fading'[1] to secure exactly the emphasis Sidney wants is a reminder of the mastery of rhetoric evident in his best poems, and possibly too of the mere obsession with it evident in his less successful ones.

This obsession was not peculiar to Sidney: to write wittily then was to write rhetorically.[2] But, if Sidney was part of a fashion,[3] he also helped to develop the fashion. He is an expert in organizing a poem by means of one dominant figure which is complicated by the use of other figures.[4] Sidney's skill was recognized by his contemporaries. Abraham Fraunce in *The Arcadian Rhetorike*[5] uses

---

9. Gen. 2. 7, Geneva Version.
1. Technically an example of *adnominatio*; see L. A. Sonnino, *A Handbook to Sixteenth-Century Rhetoric*, 1968, p. 24, where the figure is defined and exemplified.
2. W. G. Crane, op. cit., pp. 2–3.
3. V. L. Rubel, *Poetic Diction in the English Renaissance, from Skelton through Spenser*, 1941, pp. 274–5.
4. Rubel, op. cit., p. 206, gives some examples.
5. Abraham Fraunce, *The Arcadian Rhetorike*, 1588, ed. Ethel Seaton, 1950.

over one hundred extracts from the *Arcadia* and the poems,[6] and gives Sidney the honour of placing him in third place (after Homer and Virgil) in his lists of quotations.[7] John Hoskins in his *Directions for Speech and Style*[8] illustrates what he considers the best modes of speaking and writing entirely from the *Arcadia*.[9]

To appreciate the mastery of complicated and subtly varied rhetorical effects which Sidney has at his best, one could hardly do better than reread the first sonnet of *Astrophil and Stella*[1] and then look at R. L. Montgomery's detailed discussion of it.[2] In the *Arcadia* many poems show a balance and symmetry rather too obvious, at least to a modern taste. In these two stanzas the parallel between 'The marchante man' and 'The laborer' is enforced too obviously and mechanically by breaking the first five lines in each stanza after the fourth syllable, and by making each stanza change direction at the beginning of the fifth line:

> The marchante man, whome gayne dothe teache the Sea
> Where rockes do wayte, for theym the wyndes do chase,
> Beaten with waves, no sooner kennes the baye
> Wheare he was bound, to make his marting place,
>   But feare forgott, and paynes all overpaste,
>   Make present ease receave the better taste.

> The laborer, which cursed earthe up teares
> With sweatie browes, sometyme with watrie eyes,
> Ofte scorching sonne, ofte clowdie darkenes feares,
> Whyle upon chaunce, his fruite of labour lyes;
>   But harvest come, and corne in fertill store,
>   More in his owne he toyld he gladdes the more.[3]

However, the symmetry of that poem does give pleasure, if not a very profound pleasure. A poem sung by Philoclea[4] is, I think, completely unsatisfactory because its symmetry is all too obvious and, at the same time, ineffective even as symmetry. This poem is

6. Ibid., p. xxxv.   7. Ibid., p. xix.
8. John Hoskins, *Directions for Speech and Style*, composed 1599–1600, ed. H. H. Hudson, 1935.
9. Ibid., p. xv.   1. Ringler, p. 165.   2. Montgomery, pp. 84–5.
3. *O.A.* 36, Ringler, pp. 70–1.   4. *O.A.* 60, ibid., p. 84.

an example of correlative verse,[5] in which groups of words 'respond' to each other:

> 1   2   3   1   2   3
> Vertue, beawtie, and speach, did strike, wound, charme,
>
>   1   2   3   1   2   3
> My harte, eyes, eares, with wonder, love, delight:
>
>   1   2   3   1   2   3
> First, second, last, did binde, enforce, and arme,
>
>   1   2   3   1   2   3
> His workes, showes, suites, with wit, grace, and vow's might.

It goes on like this for fourteen lines. Even without the careful numbering (an indication of pride in achievement, perhaps, and certainly evidence that readers were expected to enjoy such ingenuity), no one could fail to realize roughly what was going on. The trouble is that the words are too vague, and they fail to make a strong impact on the reader, so that it is difficult even at the end of the first line to connect 'charme' with 'speach' just a few syllables back—connect it in any meaningful way, that is. This problem gets worse as the poem continues.

My objection to that poem is not that it is too clever, but that it is not clever enough: its artifice is apparent, but not successful. Anyone who objects simply to a poet's artifice being apparent would be well advised to leave Sidney alone and look elsewhere for his reading.[6] Queen Elizabeth's court was a model of artifice, ceremony, and extravagant display, and Elizabethan readers looked for, and frequently found, corresponding qualities in the poetry of the time.[7] They expected from poetry primarily, I think, 'words set in delightful proportion';[8] they expected a poem to be first a beautiful object,[9] whatever else it might be after that.

Probably Elizabethan readers were more ready than modern readers to appreciate not only what a poem was doing but also how it was doing it. Elizabethan poems generally ask for the second kind of appreciation every bit as much as for the first.[1]

5. O.A. 60, Ringler, p. 409.   6. Hunter, op. cit., p. 10.

7. Ibid., pp. 9–11. For interesting accounts of the Elizabethan love of display see Buxton, *Elizabethan Taste*, 1963; Geoffrey Tillotson, 'Elizabethan Decoration', *Essays in Criticism and Research*, 1942, pp. 5–16; F. A. Yates, 'Elizabethan Chivalry: The Romance of the Accession Day Tilts', *J.W.C.I.* xx (1957), 4–25.

8. Shepherd, p. 113.

9. Buxton, *Sir Philip Sidney and the English Renaissance*, p. 21; Tuve, p. 25.

1. Buxton, *Elizabethan Taste*, pp. 24–6.

The demand for an 'artifact . . . designed to please on grounds of its formal excellence'[2] is nowhere better seen than in the notes by 'E. K.' to Spenser's *Shepheardes Calender*.[3] These evince some knowledge of rhetoric on the part of E. K. and also a tacit assumption that the reader of his notes will have some too. Few modern readers would be able to comment on the lines

> Nowe dead he is, and lyeth wrapt in lead
> (O why should death on hym such outrage showe?)[4]

like this: 'a pretye Epanorthosis or correction',[5] or on the lines:

> I loue thilke lasse, (alas why doe I loue?)
> And am forlorne, (alas why am I lorne?)[6]

like this: 'a prety Epanorthosis in these two verses, and withall a Paronomasia or playing with the word, where he sayth (I loue thilke lasse) alas &c'.[7] Few indeed would want to be able to make such comments. It is important, however, to appreciate that it is possible and appropriate to take this kind of pleasure in the reading of Elizabethan poetry, even if the names for the devices we notice no longer spring to mind. Sidney's methods are as interesting as his effects: in football we distinguish between a mere 'goal' and a 'good' goal.

In his poetry Sidney often admits his concern with graceful expression. The line 'What sobs can give words grace my griefe to show?'[8] is typical of many. In the first poem of *Astrophil and Stella* he is seeking 'fit words to paint the blackest face of woe',[9] and in the hundred-and-fourth he is still concerned not merely with his sorrow, but with his 'sorrowe's eloquence'.[1] To be fair, he knows he should be just as concerned with what he is expressing as with how he is expressing it, and the problem is basically one of the exact adjustment of the means to the end:

Tully, when he was to drive out Catiline, as it were with a thunderbolt of eloquence, often used that figure of repetition, *Vivit. Vivit? Imo vero etiam in senatum venit*, &c. Indeed, inflamed with a well-grounded rage, he would have his words (as it were) double out of his mouth, and so do that artificially which we see men do in choler naturally.[2]

2. Tuve, p. 25. 3. Ibid., p. 34. 4. Spenser, p. 442.
5. Ibid., p. 443. 6. Ibid., p. 422. 7. Ibid., p. 423.
8. *A.S.* 93, Ringler, p. 227. 9. Ibid., p. 165.
1. Ibid., p. 233. 2. Shepherd, p. 138.

In his next sentence Sidney uses deliberately, and appropriately, a comic pun to stress the absurdity of the inappropriate use of the figure of repetition: 'And we, having noted the grace of those words, hale them in sometime to a familiar epistle, when it were too too much collar to be choleric.'[3]

Perhaps at the beginning of his 'Shepheard's tale'[4] too Sidney's constant nudging of his readers with parentheses[5] can be justified: it gives a rather comic effect, and the poem as a whole is comic:

> Behold (beholding well it doth deserve)
> They saw a maid who thitherward did runne . . .[6]

Sometimes, however, the rhetoric serves no purpose beyond itself: we feel that playing with words has become a nervous tic.[7] Examples are not hard to find:

> This mayde, thus made for joyes, ô *Pan* bemone her . . .[8]

> But cald, she came apace; a pace wherein did move
> The bande of beauties all . . .[9]

Even in *Astrophil and Stella*, where Sidney's technique is generally at its most mature, and even in some of the best poems in that sequence, we can find him tossing words about pointlessly:

> My Muse and I must you of dutie greet
> With thankes and wishes, wishing thankfully.[1]

Whole poems can be infected. The sonnet 'Now that of absence the most irksome night',[2] in which 'night' and 'day' are played on throughout, is prolix and tedious.[3]

At his best Sidney uses the rhetorical figures with taste and discrimination to enforce his meaning. Since his meaning is usually a form of persuasion, rhetoric usually goes hand in hand with dialectic.[4] The classical textbooks of rhetoric had originally

---

3. Shepherd. The word 'collar' means here 'burden'; see ibid., p. 229.
4. *O.P.* 4, Ringler, p. 242.   5. e.g., lines 17, 23, 46, 52, 58, 65, 113.
6. Lines 82–3.
7. D. G. Rees, 'Italian and Italianate Poetry', *Elizabethan Poetry* (Stratford-upon-Avon Studies 2), p. 61.
8. *O.A.* 7, Ringler, p. 17.   9. *O.A.* 73, ibid., p. 119.
1. *A.S.* 84, ibid., p. 209.   2. *A.S.* 89, ibid., p. 223.
3. Odette de Mourgues, *Metaphysical, Baroque, and Précieux Poetry*, 1953, p. 17.
4. P. A. Duhamel, 'Sidney's *Arcadia* and Elizabethan Rhetoric', *S.P.* xlv (1948), 134–50.

been intended for students of forensic oratory:[5] they were early used for the study of poetry, and the belief grew up that the poet was as concerned with persuasion as was the orator.[6] This notion survived Sidney; he takes it much for granted.[7] The strong Renaissance belief in the value of ratiocination as a means of discovering the truth,[8] and the enormous importance attached to the study of logic,[9] make it hardly surprising that so many of Sidney's poems have a logical structure. Rosemond Tuve uses Sidney to exemplify some of the ways in which poems could be organized logically.[1] Her analyses are extremely detailed; one cannot but be struck by the degree of careful thought which has gone into these poems, and the degree of thought they demand from the reader. Even a modern, without the training in logic which Sidney could quite reasonably expect from his contemporaries, must follow each stage of an argument in order to read one of these poems properly. As with the rhetoric, however, it is possible to do this without necessarily being able to attach the appropriate terms to the arguments.

Basilius singing of his love for Cleophila provides an excellent example of a poem designed to persuade.[2] Basilius is trying to persuade someone (himself, presumably, since he thinks he is alone, although he addresses Cleophila) that there is nothing disgraceful in an old man's being passionately in love. He uses a sonnet, of the form later to be known as Shakespearian, and its neat, end-stopped lines and strong, simple, confident movement are most suitable for a poem cheerfully arguing such a difficult case:

> Let not old age disgrace my high desire,
> O heavenly soule, in humaine shape conteind:
> Old wood inflam'de, doth yeeld the bravest fire,
> When yonger dooth in smoke his vertue spend.

The argument here is by analogy. Whether it is true or not is hardly relevant: it is the ingenuity which appeals. In the next quatrain Basilius again uses an argument by analogy: since Cleophila is loved for 'her'[3] white complexion, then whiteness is

---

5. Sonnino, op. cit., p. 8.
6. D. L. Clark, *Rhetoric and Poetry in the Renaissance: A Study of Rhetorical Terms in English Renaissance Literary Criticism*, 1963, pp. 99–100.
7. Shepherd, p. 139.   8. Craig, op. cit., pp. 3, 156.   9. Tuve, p. 281.
1. Ibid., pp. 312–21.   2. O.A. 15, Ringler, p. 38.
3. 'She' is, of course, Pyrocles in disguise. The situation gives a certain humour to the poem.

attractive, and his beard is white, therefore his beard may be regarded as attractive:

> Ne let white haires, which on my face doo grow,
>   Seeme to your eyes of a disgracefull hewe:
> Since whitenesse doth present the sweetest show,
>   Which makes all eyes doo honour unto you.

Then follow a couple of assertions which have almost a proverbial force:

> Old age is wise and full of constant truth;
>   Old age well stayed from raunging humor lives:

a line persuasive simply by being true:

> Old age hath knowne what ever was in youth:

and an appeal to the 'lady's' vanity:

> Old age orecome, the greater honour gives.

The sonnet is rounded off neatly by its concluding couplet: the last line repeats the first of the poem, and the couplet as a whole provides a fresh argument, and the best of all, by its ingenious play on the word 'aspire': [4]

> And to old age since you your selfe aspire,
> Let not old age disgrace my high desire.

Much of the persuasiveness of that poem comes from the cumulative effect of its arguments. There is a sense of urgency in Sidney's poems. I do not mean a solemn intensity (far from it), but rather the impression we get of travelling rapidly from one point to another, the impression of having to press on. Even his weaker poems usually have this merit. The first song in *Astrophil and Stella*, for instance, is not very impressive verbally, but the reader is swept along with it. The rhythm is rapid, and there is the cumulative effect of each stanza's being organized similarly (the first two lines asking a question with the second two answering it, the third line being identical in each stanza, and the rhymes feminine throughout, except the internal rhymes in the third line). Also

---

4. It has its Latinate meaning 'approach' (and Cleophila cannot help but approach old age) and its English meaning 'desire earnestly' (and by his pun Basilius suggests that Cleophila has this earnest desire).

there is an avoidance of monotony by a variation in the last line of each stanza:

> Doubt you to whom my Muse these notes entendeth,
> Which now my breast orecharg'd to Musicke lendeth?
> To you, to you, all song of praise is due,
> Only in you my song begins and endeth.
>
> Who hath the eyes which marrie state with pleasure,
> Who keepes the key of Nature's chiefest treasure?
> To you, to you, all song of praise is due,
> Only for you the heav'n forgate all measure. . . .[5]

This sense of continual movement and development is a more constant feature of Sidney's verse than, say, the use of complex, highly evocative, and emotionally suggestive imagery.[6]

> But now the starres with their strange course do binde
>   Me one to leave, with whome I leave my hart.
> I heare a crye of spirits faint and blind,
>   That parting thus my chiefest part I part.[7]

The third line there is perhaps the best; but it is certainly not the most typical of Sidney. Most typical of him is the word-play in the last line, and particularly the manner in which this is immediately taken up and developed in the next part of the poem:

> Part of my life, the loathed part to me,
>   Lives to impart my wearie clay some breath.
> But that good part . . .

and so on. Again, the double sestina 'Yee Gote-heard Gods, that love the grassie mountaines'[8] is effective because of the cumulative way in which the words are used. The constant repetition of the same words at the ends of the lines, but in a different order in each stanza, makes us consider them ever more fully so that we

5. Ringler, pp. 196–7.
6. Katherine Duncan-Jones, review of Kalstone, R.E.S., n.s. xvii (1966), 457; Kalstone, p. 84.
7. C.S. 20, Ringler, p. 148.   8. O.A. 71, ibid., p. 111.

take more and more meaning from them.[9] The imagery is a collection of the most obvious stage properties of the pastoral:

Strephon. Yee Gote-heard Gods, that love the grassie mountaines,
Yee Nimphes which haunt the springs in pleasant vallies,
Ye Satyrs joyde with free and quiet forrests,
Vouchsafe your silent eares to playning musique,
Which to my woes gives still an early morning:
And drawes the dolor on till wery evening.

But then the physical surroundings take on a metaphorical quality,[1] and we have '*le paysage intérieur*':

I that was once esteem'd for pleasant musique,
Am banisht now among the monstrous mountaines
Of huge despaire, and foule affliction's vallies . . .

Hart-broken so, that molehilles seeme high mountaines . . .

And not, as that last line shows, without wit.

In general Sidney's images are not so much striking in themselves as appropriate as means of conveying the argument of the poem one stage further.[2] Indeed it may be objected that sometimes his images are physically inconsistent with each other,[3] and even ludicrous in their general effect. The suggestion that in the Renaissance 'profound suggestiveness or logical subtlety is likely to displace sensuous accuracy in the images'[4] may be a justification of this procedure: it is all a question of how much 'sensuous accuracy' the reader demands or is entitled to expect. It may also be held that figures are not mixed when they are all part of the same argument.[5] In other words, the concepts which the images are there to convey must predominate in our response over the concrete suggestions of the images. We need an example. Here Stella is helping Cupid in his wars:

                    . . . her eyes
        Serve him with shot, her lips his heralds arre:
        Her breasts his tents, legs his triumphall carre:
        Her flesh his food, her skin his armour brave . . .[6]

9. This point is made in detail by William Empson, *Seven Types of Ambiguity*, 1961, pp. 34–8.
    1. Kalstone, p. 79.
    2. S. M. Cooper, *The Sonnets of Astrophel and Stella: A Stylistic Study*, 1968, p. 138.
    3. Ibid.   4. Tuve, p. 25.   5. Ibid., p. 289.   6. *A.S.* 29, Ringler, p. 179.

This may be justified on a serious level: '. . . what is most important is the ingenuity of the conception expanded by metaphor, and the unlikely but witty appropriateness of the metaphor selected.'[7] We may also argue, taking up a hint contained in the words 'unlikely' and 'witty', that the effect here is intended to be ludicrous.

It is extremely difficult to know how one should react. My feeling is that Sidney does intend his imagery here to give a touch of ludicrousness, just as he does in this line from another sonnet:

Venus is taught with *Dian's* wings to flie.[8]

Since Diana has no wings to lend, Venus is unlikely to do much flying.[9] And Sidney does know how to avoid the effect of absurdity even when he is using far-fetched images. In the song 'What toong can her perfections tell',[1] where the imagery is often reminiscent of that in the Song of Solomon, Sidney can be ingenious and witty without being ludicrous:[2]

> The bellie there gladde sight doth fill,
> Justly entitled *Cupid's* hill.
> A hill most fitte for such a master,
> A spotlesse mine of Alablaster.
> Like Alablaster faire and sleeke,
> But soft and supple satten like. . . .[3]

> There ofte steales out that round cleane foote
> This noble Cedar's pretious roote:
> In shewe and sent pale violets,
> Whose steppe on earth all beautie sets.[4]

It is not our recollection of the Song of Solomon which enables us to take those images seriously: that poem has its own comic moments for a modern Western reader:

> Your nose is like a tower of Lebanon,
> overlooking Damascus.[5]

There is good evidence, I think, that Sidney was well aware of the ludicrous possibilities latent in many images and knew how

7. Peterson, op. cit., p. 190.   8. *A.S.* 72, Ringler, p. 212.
9. Gentili, pp. 178–80.   1. *O.A.* 62, Ringler, p. 85.
2. Ibid., p. 410.   3. Lines 77–82, ibid., p. 88.
4. Lines 105–8, ibid., p. 89.   5. Song of Solomon, 7. 4, R.S.V.

they might be either suppressed or emphasized. Attaining an exact balance between the physical and the conceptual, the balance appropriate for the particular context, is a constant problem for anyone writing poetry. Of course, the writer's and the reader's notion of what is the appropriate balance will vary from time to time and place to place. This, for instance, was probably an acceptable compliment in the culture in which it was written; but no modern Western woman would take it as such:

> I compare you, my love,
>> to a mare of Pharaoh's chariots.[6]

What is basically the same comparison may, however, form a compliment in our own culture, if the poet suppresses inappropriate physical connotations and concentrates the reader's attention on the required concepts:

> But even at the starting-post, all sleek and new,
> I saw the wildness in her. . . .[7]

To return to Sidney, the line 'My mouth too tender is for thy hard bit',[8] while not without an appropriate touch of humour, is not saying 'I am a horse.' Then, in another poem,

> . . . unbitted thought
> Doth fall to stray . . .[9]

is not funny at all. In the sonnet where Astrophil rides his horse while Cupid rides him the basic concept is intentionally ridiculous:

> I on my horse, and *Love* on me doth trie
>> Our horsemanships, while by strange worke I prove
>> A horseman to my horse, a horse to *Love* . . .[1]

Consequently, the comparison is worked out in detail to emphasize this ridiculousness:

> The raines wherewith my Rider doth me tie,
>> Are humbled thoughts, which bit of Reverence move,
>> Curb'd in with feare, but with guilt bosse above
> Of Hope, which makes it seeme faire to the eye.

6. Song of Solomon, i. 9.
7. 'A Bronze Head', *The Collected Poems of W. B. Yeats*, 1950, p. 382.
8. *A.S.* 4, Ringler, p. 166.   9. *A.S.* 38, ibid., p. 183.
1. *A.S.* 49, ibid., p. 189.

The method and the effect are very similar to those in a stanza from the *Faerie Queene*; Marinell, previously impervious to the charms of women, falls in love with Florimell when he hears her lament her love for him:

> Thus whilst his stony heart with tender ruth
> Was toucht, and mighty courage mollifide,
> Dame *Venus* sonne that tameth stubborne youth
> With iron bit, and maketh him abide,
> Till like a victor on his backe he ride,
> Into his mouth his maystring bridle threw,
> That made him stoupe, till he did him bestride:
> Then gan he make him tread his steps anew,
> And learne to loue, by learning louers paines to rew.[2]

People often seem to be doubtful whether Spenser has much sense of humour.[3] Only the most obtuse could have any such doubts about Sidney; but I think the pervasiveness of his humour is frequently underestimated.

It is interesting to compare 'I on my horse . . .' with Shakespeare's sonnet 'How heavy do I journey on the way'.[4] Sidney's poem shows the development of a comparison to accord with a way of looking at experience which is traditional, and everything seems to have been worked out carefully beforehand. With Shakespeare, on the other hand, we have the impression of something being worked out as the poem develops; Shakespeare seems to take things as they come and see where they lead him.[5] This is one of the main differences between Sidney and Shakespeare.[6] Another way of putting it is to say that Sidney's method is often allegorical, while Shakespeare's leads naturally to metaphor:

> The beast that bears me, tiréd with my woe,
> Plods dully on, to bear that weight in me,
> As if by some instinct the wretch did know
> His rider loved not speed being made from thee:
> The bloody spur cannot provoke him on,
> That sometimes anger thrusts into his hide,
> Which heavily he answers with a groan,
> More sharp to me than spurring to his side . . .

2. *F.Q.* IV.xii.13, Spenser, p. 273.
3. e.g., William Nelson, *The Poetry of Edmund Spenser*, 1965, p. 138.
4. Wilson, ed. cit., no. 50, p. 27. 5. Lever, p. 205. 6. Danby, op. cit., p. 72.

We have very little idea of how either writer went to work; but Sidney's poems read as though they are the result of 'ordering at the first what should be at the last'.[7] Significantly, Sidney is usually very successful at rounding his sonnets off,[8] while the concluding couplets of Shakespeare's are sometimes weak.[9]

To say this is not in any way to deny the superiority of Shakespeare at his best over Sidney at his best. Indeed, the use of such terms as 'orderly' to describe Sidney's poems,[1] the statement that they express 'the vision of rational self-control',[2] and the comparison of the calm and measured way in which they are constructed with the manner of George Herbert[3]—all imply Sidney's limitations. At their best it is part of their charm, and at their worst it is a weakness that his poems are so evidently 'peizing each syllable of each word by just proportion according to the dignity of the subject'.[4]

In the *Arcadia* particularly, the poems seem like set performances.[5] When the speaker is bewailing his hard lot, the very neatness and 'effectiveness' of his manner leads often to a strange sort of complacency:

> Transformd in shew, but more transformd in minde,
> I cease to strive, with double conquest foild:
> For (woe is me) my powers all I finde
> With outward force and inward treason spoild.
>
> For from without came to mine eyes the blowe,
> Whereto mine inward thoughts did faintly yeeld;
> Both these conspird poore Reason's overthrowe;
> False in my selfe, thus have I lost the field.[6]

7. Shepherd, p. 133.
8. J. G. Scott, *Les Sonnets Élisabéthains: Les Sources et l'Apport Personnel*, 1929, p. 50.
9. Auden, intro. to *William Shakespeare: The Sonnets*, ed. William Burto, 1964, p. xxv.
1. Craik, op. cit., p. 11.
2. Rudenstine, p. 56. This is a comment on the *Arcadia* poems.
3. L. L. Martz, *The Poetry of Meditation: A Study in English Religious Literature of the Seventeenth Century*, 1955, p. 267.
4. Shepherd, p. 103.   5. Rudenstine, p. 60.
6. *O.A.* 2, Ringler, p. 11. See also *O.A.* 17, 38, 39, ibid., pp. 39, 72.

'Poore Reason's overthrowe' is accepted a little too comfortably.
When Sidney is expressing thoughts in themselves more cheerful,
then this manner is more appropriate:

> Since nature's workes be good, and death doth serve
> As nature's worke: why should we feare to dye?
> Since feare is vaine, but when it may preserve,
> Why should we feare that which we cannot flye?[7]

A brisk, balanced, and self-confident manner is just what this poem
needs. However, even the poems I have described as complacent
have their own kind of charm. They appeal to a reader's delight in
symmetry and harmony, even if (perhaps because) they seem far
removed from extra-artistic experience. As Dorus puts it in
Sidney's self-deprecating way:

> Silly shepheard's poore pype, when his harsh sound testifis
>   our woes,
> Into the faire looker on, pastime, not passion, enters.[8]

Sonnets by Sidney and Shakespeare on similar themes[9] high-
light the difference in their approach. 'Thou blind man's marke,
thou foole's selfe chosen snare' is one of Sidney's finest sonnets,
no one could describe it as complacent, and most people would,
I think, agree that it uses rhetoric most effectively as a means and
not as an end. Nevertheless, in comparison with Shakespeare, it is
remarkable just how neatly Sidney has things worked out:

> Thou blind man's marke, thou foole's selfe chosen snare,
> Fond fancie's scum, and dregs of scattred thought,
> Band of all evils, cradle of causelesse care,
> Thou web of will, whose end is never wrought . . .

In Shakespeare, lust is far more powerful and frightening, not
because his artistry is less, of course, but because it is greater:

7. *O.A.* 77, ibid., p. 131.   8. *O.A.* 13, lines 40–1, ibid., p. 32.
  9. Symonds, op. cit., p. 153, mentions the resemblance between 'Thou blind
man's marke, thou foole's selfe chosen snare', *C.S.* 31, Ringler, p. 161, and Shakespeare's Sonnet 129, 'Th'expense of spirit in a waste of shame', ed. cit., p. 67, and
between 'Leave me ô Love, which reachest but to dust', *C.S.* 32, Ringler, p. 161,
and Shakespeare's Sonnet 146, 'Poor soul the centre of my sinful earth', ed. cit., p.
75.

> Th' expense of spirit in a waste of shame
> Is lust in action, and till action, lust
> Is perjured, murd'rous, bloody full of blame,
> Savage, extreme, rude, cruel, not to trust . . .

The difference is not simply one of style. Shakespeare in this sonnet, as so often in his work, shows a deep awareness of the dark and tragic side of human nature; his poem ends:

> All this the world well knows yet none knows well,
> To shun the heaven that leads men to this hell.

That is skilfully done, with its alliteration on 'w', its play on 'well knows' and 'knows well', and the sharp contrast (enforced by alliteration) between 'heaven' and 'hell'; but our sense of his despair is stronger than our sense of his skill in expressing it. Sidney never conveys in his poems such a deep sense of tragedy, and this sonnet of his ends on a note of triumph:

> But yet in vaine thou hast my ruine sought,
> In vaine thou madest me to vaine things aspire,
> In vaine thou kindlest all thy smokie fire;

> For vertue hath this better lesson taught,
> Within my selfe to seeke my onelie hire:
> Desiring nought but how to kill desire.

The more obvious rhetoric (the repetition of 'in vaine', the play on 'in vaine' and 'vaine things', and the play on 'Desiring' and 'desire' with its striking shift of meaning) is part of the triumph. Finally, Shakespeare's concluding couplet, while certainly not one of his weak ones, is typically thrown almost casually over his shoulder (its casualness makes it the more despairing), while Sidney's last line is clearly the most powerful in the poem. At their worst, Shakespeare's final couplets seem to be there simply because he could not get out of including them.[1] Sidney sometimes makes us suspect that the first thirteen lines had to be written for the sake of the last.[2]

I do not wish, in laying a greater stress on the orderliness and neat build-up of the arguments in Sidney's poems, to imply that his imagery lacks force or subtlety. His tact and judgment can be

1. e.g., the final couplets of two of his best sonnets: nos. 110, 111, ed. cit., pp. 57–8.
2. e.g., *A.S.* 40 and 48, Ringler, pp. 184, 188.

best seen, perhaps, when the material of his images is most commonplace. Among the most commonplace material available to
him was, of course, classical myth. Knowledge of classical myth
was then so widespread, and it lent itself so readily to metaphorical
use,[3] that it was possible for Sidney to create quite a striking effect
by a mere glancing reference or allusion. Thom Gunn finds the
resemblance between the moon and the lover in Sidney's sonnet
'With how sad steps, ô Moone, thou climb'st the skies'[4] 'tenuous';
he says it 'depends entirely on the fact that the moon is slow in its
movement, and therefore seems sad, like a sad lover'.[5] The slow-
ness of the moon's movement is certainly relevant; but so too is
the slight, scarcely hinted at, recollection of the myth of Endy-
mion and Phoebe, so easy for a modern to miss.

'That busie archer' in the same sonnet is an allusion which it
would be difficult to miss even nowadays and, as the word 'That'
suggests, Sidney is implying that the archer is an old acquaintance
of the reader as well as of Astrophil. Some of Sidney's best uses of
classical myth are of this kind:[6]

> Nymph of the gard'n, where all beauties be:
> Beauties which do in excellencie passe
> His who till death lookt in a watrie glasse,
> Or hers whom naked the *Trojan* boy did see.
> Sweet gard'n Nymph, which keepes the Cherrie tree,
> Whose fruit doth farre th'*Esperian* tast surpasse . . .[7]

Narcissus and Helen are present all the more forcibly because they
are alluded to, and not named. The attentive reader notices also
that the comparison of Stella to the proverbial personification of
self-love is not entirely on the grounds of their common beauty,
and so not entirely a compliment; at the same time, the image is
well controlled and it would be wrong to call the comparison an
insult. It is similar with the comparison to Helen; again, Stella and
she have beauty in common, but Helen is famous also for her
extra-marital adventures. There is a touch of envy, and perhaps

3. Tuve, p. 162.   4. *A.S.* 31, Ringler, p. 180.
5. *Selected Poems of Fulke Greville*, ed. Thom Gunn, 1968, p. 17.
6. Robertson, op. cit., p. 128: 'The most potent classical allusions are those in
which the character alluded to is not named: "the busie archer" of Sonnet 31; the
unnamed presence of Orpheus in Sonnet 36, or of Narcissus in 82; the comparison
of Astrophel to Prometheus in Sonnet 14 . . .'
7. *A.S.* 82, Ringler, pp. 207-8.

also of hope, in the mention of 'the *Trojan* boy'. If the reference to
'th'*Esperian* tast' calls to mind Dido, who was also unfaithful to
her husband (admittedly after his death),[8] then so much the better.
The resemblance must not be pushed too far (Stella nowhere
contemplates suicide, and Astrophil never shows any signs of
sailing away); but then Sidney does not push it too far.

Sidney can refer briefly to '*Phenix Stella's* state'[9] to suggest
Stella's uniqueness. The reader is expected to take that notion
from the reference and ignore what is irrelevant: Stella is clearly a
lady not for burning. Similarly, the line 'No lovely *Paris* made thy
Hellen his'[1] allows the suggestion that an unlovely, and unloved,
Menelaus did. The names of figures from classical myth are often
used in this way, indicating a type of person:

> On silly me do not the burthen lay,
>   Of all the grave conceits your braine doth breed;
>   But find some *Hercules* to beare, in steed
> Of *Atlas* tyr'd, your wisdome's heav'nly sway.[2]

Both these names are still used of strong men; but there is more to
Sidney's lines than that. There is a reference to the story in which
Hercules deputizes for Atlas for a while and holds the heavens on
his shoulders. It is a comic story, for Atlas intends to get rid of the
heavens for good, and Hercules restores them to their usual sup-
porter by a trick. Recollection of this comedy is fitting, for Astrophil is mocking himself as '*Atlas* tyr'd'.

The ease with which the literal sky of the myth becomes 'your
wisdome's heav'nly sway' shows how readily myths could be
allegorized. This is one of the points which come out strongly in
the *Apology*:

So, as Amphion was said to move stones with his poetry to build
Thebes, and Orpheus to be listened to by beasts—indeed stony and
beastly people—so among the Romans were Livius Andronicus and
Ennius.[3]

8. See *Aeneid* iv, 480–8, with an English translation by H. R. Fairclough, 1965, i,
428.
9. *A.S.* 92, Ringler, p. 225.   1. *A.S.* 33, ibid., p. 181.
2. *A.S.* 51, ibid., p. 190.
3. Shepherd, p. 96. The use of Amphion and Orpheus to illustrate the power of
music and poetry was a commonplace; see ibid., p. 147, and also *A.S.*, Song 3,
Ringler, p. 208.

The poet is 'the right popular philosopher',[4] and his title to this name is justified by reference to the fables of Aesop, which are 'pretty allegories'.[5] The poet comes 'with a tale',[6] and his readers will be glad

> to hear the tales of Hercules, Achilles, Cyrus, and Aeneas; and, hearing them, must needs hear the right description of wisdom, valour, and justice; which, if they had been barely, that is to say philosophically, set out, they would swear they be brought to school again.[7]

Whether the characters spoken of are mythical or historical, they are seen as representing abstract qualities, and that is allegory.[8] Sidney says quite explicitly that we should go to poetry for 'things not affirmatively but allegorically and figuratively written'.[9]

This is an approach not entirely uncongenial to a modern, and it is perhaps only Sidney's emphasis which distinguishes his attitude from ours. People in the Renaissance took classical myths no more literally than we do; the myths were important to them for the allegorical bearing they so obviously had on human experience.[1] It is the same now. No one looking at a cap-badge of the Royal Corps of Signals takes it literally, as an indication that soldiers in that corps go naked but for wings on head and feet: the figure of Mercury is immediately translated into the notion of 'communications', allegorized, in fact.

The pastoral form was particularly suitable for allegory; one might even say that it necessarily implied allegory and 'hiding royall bloud full oft in rurall vaine'.[2] The shepherds are not shepherds, but poets often, and sometimes kings or bishops;[3] the shepherd Dorus in the *Arcadia* is really the disguised Musidorus, prince of Thessalia. If we bear this in mind, the sudden metamorphosis of the courtly Astrophil into a shepherd, and of Stella into

---

4. Shepherd, p. 109.   5. Ibid.   6. Ibid., p. 113.
7. Ibid., pp. 113–14.
8. Lewis, *The Allegory of Love: A Study in Medieval Tradition*, 1953, p. 322: 'Allegory consists in giving an imagined body to the immaterial . . .'
9. Shepherd, p. 124.
1. Craig, op. cit., p. 66; W. L. Renwick, *Edmund Spenser: An Essay on Renaissance Poetry*, 1925, pp. 142–5.
2. *A.S.* 6, Ringler, p. 167.   3. Renwick, op. cit., pp. 76–7.

a shepherdess,[4] comes as no very great surprise.[5] In the *Apology* it is as allegory that the pastoral is justified:

> It is then the Pastoral poem which is misliked? For perchance where the hedge is lowest they will soonest leap over. Is the poor pipe disdained, which sometime out of Meliboeus' mouth can show the misery of people under hard lords or ravening soldiers? And again, by Tityrus, what blessedness is derived to them that lie lowest from the goodness of them that sit highest; sometimes, under the pretty tales of wolves and sheep, can include the whole considerations of wrongdoing and patience. . . .[6]

The names given to the characters in the *Arcadia* frequently suggest abstract qualities,[7] as indeed do the names 'Stella' and 'Astrophil'. I am not suggesting that the *Arcadia*, still less *Astrophil and Stella*, should be read as full-blown allegories in the manner of the *Faerie Queene*, but simply that there are tendencies that way in both. This fact, and the general inclination at the time to read everything as allegory,[8] make me very doubtful that Sidney had Spenser particularly in mind when he wrote:

> You that with allegorie's curious frame,
>   Of other's children changelings use to make,
>   With me those paines for God's sake do not take:
> I list not dig so deepe for brasen fame.
> When I say '*Stella*', I do meane the same
>   Princesse of Beautie, for whose only sake
>   The raines of *Love* I love . . .[9]

Sidney is not talking about Spenser's, or any other writer's, technique; he is concerned with the reader's way of reading, and warning him that he must for once give up the habit of allegorizing what he reads. There is the typically self-deprecating implication too that the sonnets are not worthy of the sort of treatment given to, say, the *Aeneid*. We are told that Stella is not an abstraction but a real woman;[1] this does not imply any dislike of allegory

---

4. *A.S.*, Song 9, Ringler, p. 221.

5. See also *O.P.* 6 and 7, ibid., pp. 260, 262.   6. Shepherd, p. 116.

7. For a list of them, with meanings, see Ringler, p. 382. Buxton suggests a correction of one of the meanings in his review of Ringler, *R.E.S.*, N.S. xv (1964), 202.

8. Nelson, op. cit., pp. 116–30.

9. *A.S.* 28, Ringler, pp. 178–9. It is suggested, in Lever, p. 75, that this refers to Spenser.

1. *A.S.* 28, Ringler, pp. 178–9.

in itself. This sonnet has in full measure that enigmatic quality which, perhaps as much as anything else, accounts for Sidney's charm and for an extraordinary number of books and articles. Stella is a real woman, yes; but to call her 'Stella' is to invite the very kind of reading which this sonnet disclaims. Also, after seeming to be about to do so, Sidney does not say who this real woman is. The reader is being teased.

There are poems which can be read only as allegory, such as the fable 'As I my little flocke on *Ister* banke'[2] with its relevance to government. The tendency to allegorize is likely to break out at any moment; the game of barley-break[3] positively asks for it:

> Then couples three be streight allotted there,
> They of both ends the middle two doe flie,
> The two that in mid place, Hell called were,
> Must strive with waiting foot, and watching eye
> To catch of them, and them to hell to beare,
> That they, aswell as they, Hell may supplie:
> > Like some which seeke to salve their blotted name
> > With others' blott, till all do tast of shame.
> There may you see, soone as the middle two
> Do coupled towards either couple make,
> They false and fearfull do their hands undoe,
> Brother his brother, frend doth frend forsake,
> Heeding himselfe, cares not how fellow doe,
> But of a straunger mutuall help doth take:
> > As perjur'd cowards in adversity
> > With sight of feare from frends to fremb'd do flie.
> These sports shepheards deviz'd such faults to show.[4]

The sixth sonnet of *Astrophil and Stella*[5] mocks the use of mythological machinery, but the very next sonnet has Cupid resting in Stella's black eyes:

> . . . she minding *Love* should be
> Placed ever there, gave him this mourning weed,
> To honor all their deaths, who for her bleed.[6]

2. *O.A.* 66, Ringler, p. 98.
4. *O.P.* 4, lines 225-41, ibid., p. 248.
6. *A.S.* 7, ibid., p. 168.

3. For the rules see ibid., p. 495.
5. Ibid., p. 167.

The sonnet after that is a short allegorical narrative which explains why Cupid cannot leave Astrophil's heart:

> *Love* borne in *Greece*, of late fled from his native place,
> Forc'd by a tedious proofe, that Turkish hardned hart,
> Is no fit marke to pierce with his fine pointed dart . . .[7]

Cupid, or Love (and the frequent use of this abstract word as a name for him is an indication of how he is allegorically conceived),[8] is likely to pop up anywhere in Sidney's poems.[9] He is an engaging person, playful and powerful, and at the same time the embodiment of a human emotion:

> *Cupid* the wagg, that lately conquer'd had
> Wise Counsellors, stout Captaines, puissant Kings,
> And ti'de them fast to leade his triumph badd,
> Glutted with them now plaies with meanest things.
> So oft in feasts with costly chaunges cladd
> To crammed mawes a spratt new Stomake brings.[1]

In the literary climate of those times, perhaps it is not Sidney's use of allegory so much as his ability to write straight fiction which should be stressed. The poem 'A neighbor mine not long ago there was'[2]—a tale of a jealous countryman, his wife, a shepherd-courtier and, naturally, the cuckolding of the countryman— invites comparison with Spenser's tale of Malbecco, Hellenore, and Paridell.[3] In both stories the adultery is treated as a joke. In Sidney the courtier

> . . . stayd untill the goodman was departed,
> Then gave he him the blow which never smarted.[4]

In Spenser, Hellenore is seen by Malbecco, after Paridell has deserted her, among satyrs:

> At night, when all they went to sleepe, he vewd,
> Whereas his louely wife emongst them lay,
> Embraced of a *Satyre* rough and rude,

---

7. *A.S.* 8, Ringler, p. 168.
8. 'By *Argus* got on *Io*, then a cow' according to *O.A.* 8, ibid., p. 21.
9. e.g., to mention only some sonnets in which he is a leading figure in a narrative, *A.S.* 11, 12, 13, 17, 20, 73, ibid., pp. 170–1, 173, 174, 203.
1. *O.P.* 4, lines 129–34, ibid., p. 245.
2. *O.A.* 64, ibid., p. 94.   3. *F.Q.* iii.ix–x, Spenser, pp. 188–200.
4. Lines 119–20, Ringler, p. 97.

Who all the night did minde his ioyous play:
Nine times he heard him come aloft ere day,
That all his hart with gealosie did swell;
But yet that nights ensample did bewray,
That not for nought his wife them loued so well,
When one so oft a night did ring his matins bell.[5]

There the resemblance ends. Sidney's tale remains an everyday story of country folk; but Spenser's Malbecco has virtually changed into the goat which his name implies he is like:

. . . out of his bush
Vpon his hands and feete he crept full light,
And like a Gote emongst the Gotes did rush,
That through the helpe of his faire hornes on hight,
And misty dampe of misconceiuing night,
And eke through likenesse of his gotish beard,
He did the better counterfeite aright:
So home he marcht emongst the horned heard,
That none of all the *Satyres* him espyde or heard.[6]

Sidney tags his tale with a moral, it is true:

Thus may you see, the jealous wretch was made
The Pandare of the thing, he most did feare,
Take heed therefore, how you ensue that trade,
Least that some markes of jealousie you beare.
For sure, no jealousie can that prevent,
Whereto two parties once be full content.[7]

But Spenser's Malbecco in the end turns into the very fault which has caused all his troubles; he is

. . . woxen so deform'd, that he has quight
Forgot he was a man, and *Gealosie* is hight.[8]

Although it is true that by 'poetry' in his *Apology* Sidney means all imaginative literature,[9] it is also true that he has poetry, in our sense of the word, particularly in mind in that treatise; his mention

5. *F.Q.* III.x.48, Spenser, p. 198.   6. *F.Q.* III.x.47, ibid.
7. Lines 121–6, Ringler, p. 97.   8. *F.Q.* III.x.60, Spenser, p. 200.
9. Shepherd, p. 103: '. . . verse being but an ornament and no cause to Poetry, since there have been many most excellent poets that never versified, and now swarm many versifiers that need never answer to the name of poets.'

of music supports my belief that he was, in the most famous passage of all, thinking of poetry in our sense. The poet

cometh to you with words set in delightful proportion, either accompanied with, or prepared for, the well enchanting skill of music; and with a tale forsooth he cometh unto you, with a tale which holdeth children from play, and old men from the chimney corner.[1]

This tale will be, to some extent at least, a fictional one. Indeed, it is one of the chief advantages of literature that the writer is not imprisoned like 'the historian in his bare *was*':[2]

And do they not know that a tragedy is tied to the laws of Poesy, and not of History; not bound to follow the story, but, having liberty, either to feign a quite new matter, or to frame the history to the most tragical conveniency?[3]

Sidney is in no doubt of the need for literature to improve on life. In Plato, for instance,

all standeth upon dialogues wherein he feigneth many honest burgesses of Athens to speak of such matters, that, if they had been set on the rack, they would never have confessed them; besides his poetical describing the circumstances of their meetings, as the well ordering of a banquet, the delicacy of a walk, with interlacing mere tales, as Gyges' Ring, and others, which who knoweth not to be flowers of poetry did never walk into Apollo's garden.[4]

The poet, 'freely ranging only within the zodiac of his own wit',[5] improves on everyday life by revealing, through his fiction, deeper truths than everyday life can reveal.[6] He goes one better than nature:

Nature never set forth the earth in so rich tapestry as divers poets have done; neither with pleasant rivers, fruitful trees, sweet-smelling flowers, nor whatsoever else may make the too much loved earth more lovely. Her world is brazen, the poets only deliver a golden.[7]

That by itself may seem to be a prescription for mere sensuous delight. If it does, Sidney soon disabuses us. The poet, he says, is able in his fiction to reveal moral qualities, to make them more

1. Shepherd, p. 113.   2. Ibid., p. 110.   3. Ibid., p. 135.
4. Ibid., p. 97.   5. Ibid., p. 100.
6. Maurice Evans, *English Poetry in the Sixteenth Century*, 1967, p. 157.
7. Shepherd, p. 100.

evident than they are in nature, and so give us a better opportunity to acquire them ourselves:

... so far substantially it worketh, not only to make a Cyrus, which had been but a particular excellency as Nature might have done, but to bestow a Cyrus upon the world to make many Cyruses, if they will learn aright why and how that maker made him.[8]

We seem to be some way towards an answer to the question touched on at the beginning of this chapter: does Sidney's own poetry support his argument in the *Apology* that the poet's aim in writing is to make men 'know that goodness whereunto they are moved'?[9] In his very interesting discussions of Sidney's theory of poetry A. C. Hamilton is right, I think, to stress the importance Sidney attaches to fiction and to its moral value:

Sidney gives poetry a power beyond moving which the earlier critics allowed: it moves *upwards*, and so supplements the working of grace. By re-creating its vision of the golden world, the reader may be moved to that virtuous action through which he may be redeemed.[1]

A slight doubt lingers, however. Is not the practice of this theory seen more obviously in Spenser than in Sidney?[2] Sidney certainly defends the poet well from the charge of being a liar: 'Now for the poet, he nothing affirms, and therefore never lieth.'[3] But how far can Sidney's theory be stretched to justify on moral grounds lyrics which seem sometimes amoral,[4] and sometimes even immoral?[5] I think we must admit that here Sidney's practice is more sophisticated than his theory—not a bad thing for a poet, after all. All the same, one of the justifications which a modern might offer—that such poetry enlarges the imagination, or makes us more aware of reality so that informed moral judgment becomes more possible—seems to be anticipated at one point by Sidney in the effects which he attributes to all learning of which

8. Ibid., p. 101.   9. Ibid., p. 103.

1. *The Structure of Allegory in The Faerie Queene*, 1964, p. 27. The whole of the first chapter of this book, 'The Nature of Spenser's Allegory' (pp. 1–43), is relevant. Two earlier discussions of Sidney's theory by the same writer, which use material later taken into that chapter, are 'Sidney and Agrippa', R.E.S., n.s. vii (1956), 151–7, and 'Sidney's Idea of the "Right Poet" ', C.L. ix (1957), 51–9.

2. In *The Structure of Allegory* Hamilton is interpreting Sidney's theory for its relevance to the *Faerie Queene*.

3. Shepherd, p. 123.

4. e.g., *C.S.* 4, Ringler, p. 137. See also pp. 1–2 above.

5. e.g., *A.S.* 75, ibid., p. 204.

poetry is a part: 'This purifying of wit, this enriching of memory, enabling of judgment, and *enlarging of conceit*, which we commonly call learning . . .'[6]

One of the qualities we enjoy in a writer of fiction is a sense of the dramatic, and we do find this in Sidney. We may find it within a poem, or in the relation of one poem to another. The fable 'As I my little flock on *Ister* banke'[7] has a dramatic quality perhaps not immediately apparent. We should read it in its context in the *Old Arcadia* where it is one of a group of poems of which the others are about marriage. Its discussion of the best way of governing a state then becomes relevant to the other poems' discussion of government in marriage.[8] It comes out strongly against tyranny in the state, and the poem 'A neighbor mine not long agoe there was'[9] shows the trouble caused by tyranny in marriage.

Again, the little lyric 'My true love hath my hart, and I have his',[1] while it certainly has a value of its own apart from its context[2] (so that it is not surprising that it has often been anthologized), does gain an extra dimension when seen within its context. There it is part of an elaborate piece of humorous deception: Musidorus, who wishes to get Miso out of the way in order to elope with Pamela, tells Miso that he has heard a young shepherdess singing this song to Miso's husband and arranging an assignation with him. This gives the apparently very simple lyric more than a touch of mockery.[3]

A poem which loses most of its point if its context is not known is the song of Dametas 'Now thanked be the great God *Pan*'.[4] The cowardly Dametas, who should be guarding Pamela, hides in a bush when she is attacked by a bear, while his servant Dorus saves Pamela. Then Dametas emerges and, with a patent sophistry which makes him look all the more ridiculous, attributes the best of the glory to himself:

> Now thanked be the great God *Pan*,
> That thus preserves my loved life:
> Thanked be I that keepe a man,

6. Shepherd, p. 104. The italics are mine.   7. *O.A.* 66, Ringler, p. 98.
8. Ibid., p. 412.   9. *O.A.* 64, ibid., p. 94.
1. *O.A.* 45, ibid., p. 75.
2. J. Grundy, review of Ringler, *M.L.R.* lviii (1963), 552.
3. Ringler, pp. xl–xli.   4. *O.A.* 5, ibid., p. 13.

> Who ended hath this fearefull strife:
>   So if my man must praises have,
>   What then must I that keepe the knave?
>
> For as the Moone the eie doth please,
> With gentle beames not hurting sight:
> Yet hath sir Sunne the greatest praise,
> Because from him doth come her light:
>   So if my man must praises have,
>   What then must I that keepe the knave?

There is a further complication, that the 'knave' Dorus is really the prince Musidorus in disguise, serving to make Dametas still more ridiculous.

There is obvious drama in the many poems from the *Arcadia* which are conversations. Typical are the argument between Reason and Passion,[5] the ingenious debate between Geron and Histor on the advisability of getting married,[6] and the argument between Geron and Philisides.[7] This last starts in a vain attempt by Geron to cheer Philisides up, continues with the old man warning Philisides against allowing himself to be in love, and develops into a heated argument between youth and age. Philisides' mockery of old men is sharp:

> And herein most their folly vaine appeares
> That since they still alledge, *When they were yong*:
> It shews they fetch their wit from youthfull yeares
> Like beast for sacrifice, where save the tong
> And belly nought is left. . . .[8]

But Geron has had his moments:

> Whome wit makes vaine, or blinded with his eyes,
> What counsell can prevaile, or light give light?
> Since all his force against himselfe he tries.
> Then each conceit that enters in by sight,
> Is made, forsooth, a Jurate of his woes,
> Earth, sea, ayre, fire, heav'n, hell, and gastly sprite.
> Then cries to sencelesse things, which neither knowes
> What ayleth thee, and if they knew thy minde
> Would scorne in man (their king) such feeble shows.[9]

5. *O.A.* 27, ibid., p. 46.   6. *O.A.* 67, ibid., p. 103.   7. *O.A.* 9, ibid., p. 22.
8. Lines 78–82, ibid., p. 24.   9. Lines 35–43, ibid., p. 23.

Histor's summing-up does not give much credit to either, and we are left without any firm conclusions having been reached:

> Thus may you see, howe youthe estemeth aige
> And never hathe therof arightelye deemde
> Whyle hote desyres do Raigne in fancie's rage
> Till aige it self do make it self esteemde.[1]

Presenting his material in dramatic form is one of Sidney's ways of showing its complexity and avoiding any neat resolution which would oversimplify this complexity. This is true enough of the poems in the *Arcadia*,[2] and *Astrophil and Stella* is even more dramatic, playful, and humorous.[3]

His lightness and playfulness seem to me qualities which distinguish Sidney's poems sharply from those of his friend Greville to which they have often been compared.[4] Greville is not always without wit,[5] but his temper is stern[6] and he is usually stodgy and heavy-handed compared with Sidney. It is significant that George Williamson, after comparing Greville's 'In the time when herbs and flowers'[7] with Sidney's 'In a grove most rich of shade',[8] should 'find Greville worthy of more *serious* interest than . . . Sidney'.[9] Yvor Winters finds Sidney at his best when he is developing his 'most *serious* themes'.[1] Fred Inglis, who is inclined to regard Greville as a better poet than Sidney,[2] is so apparently because he thinks of Sidney as 'incomplete and trivial'.[3] Like Yvor Winters, Fred Inglis sees Sidney as most successful when he is treating 'urgent themes'.[4] Such 'urgent themes' are to be found in Sidney's versions of the Psalms,[5] of which Fred Inglis includes a

---

1. Lines 138–41, ibid., p. 26.   2. Kalstone, pp. 47–8.   3. Grundy, loc. cit.
4. Gunn, ed. cit., pp. 16–19, 20, 26; J. M. Purcell, 'Sidney's *Astrophel and Stella* and Greville's *Caelica*', *P.M.L.A.* 1 (1935), 413–22; George Williamson, 'The Convention of *The Exstasie*', *Seventeenth Century Contexts*, 1960, pp. 63–77.
5. See, e.g., 'Oh wearisome condition of humanity!', Thom Gunn, ed. cit., p. 149.
6. Buxton, *Sir Philip Sidney and the English Renaissance*, p. 110.
7. Gunn, ed. cit., *Caelica*, lxxv, p. 101.   8. *A.S.*, Song 8, Ringler, p. 217.
9. Williamson, op. cit., p. 77. My italics.
1. 'The Sixteenth Century Lyric in England', an essay in three parts, *P.C.* (February, March, April 1939), part iii, p. 39. My italics.
2. Inglis, op. cit., p. 71.   3. Ibid., p. 73.
4. *English Poetry 1550–1660*, 1965, p. 29.
5. Sidney made versions of the first forty-three, printed in their earlier form by Ringler, pp. 270–337. J. C. A. Rathmell, *The Psalms of Sir Philip Sidney and the Countess of Pembroke*, 1963, prints Sidney's versions as revised by his sister. For a brief history of English metrical psalms see Hallett Smith, 'English Metrical Psalms in the Sixteenth Century and their Literary Significance', *H.L.Q.* ix (1945–6), 249–71.

surprising number (there are three, and even one would be a surprising number) in his anthology *English Poetry 1550–1660*.[6] Some consider that his sister's versions are better than Sidney's,[7] which is no very great compliment to her. Sidney's are not generally liked[8] and, although they may be excused as possibly early work,[9] we certainly cannot do what Ruskin does and simply say, when we do not like one of them, that it is probably not by Sidney at all.[1] The very existence of Sidney's versions, written with a flair for tedium, remains a mystery to me.

Perhaps the subject forbade humour; and Sidney is usually at his best when his sense of humour has full play. This can be seen easily if we compare the seventeenth sonnet of *Astrophil and Stella*[2] with the thirteenth of Greville's *Caelica*.[3] In both poems Cupid offends his mother by failing to bring Mars up to scratch, and as a consequence loses the use of his bow and arrows; but what in Greville is vague—

> And in his blindness wandereth many places,
> Till his foe Absence, hath him prisoner gotten,
> Who breaks his arrows, bow and wings defaces,
> Keeps him till he his boy's play hath forgotten,

—vague because it is hard to imagine why Absence should be able to do these things—is in Sidney a sharply drawn scene of domestic strife:

> But she in chafe him from her lap did shove,
> Brake bow, brake shafts, while *Cupid* weeping sate:
> Till that his grandame *Nature* pittying it,
> Of *Stella's* browes made him two better bowes,
> And in her eyes of arrowes infinit.

6. Inglis, *English Poetry 1550–1660*, pp. 66–70. He prints them as revised by Sidney's sister.

7. Muir, *Introduction to Elizabethan Literature*, 1967, p. 38; Rathmell, op. cit., pp. xi, xxi, xxvi.

8. Muir, *Sir Philip Sidney*, p. 7; M. W. Wallace, *The Life of Sir Philip Sidney*, 1915, p. 324.

9. Rudenstine, p. 286; Thompson, 'Sir Philip and the Forsaken Iamb', *K.R.* xx (1958), 96.

1. 'Rock Honeycomb', *Works*, xxxi, 1907, 143, 152.   2. Ringler, p. 173.

3. Gunn, ed. cit., p. 53.

Greville finishes by mentioning Cupid's playfulness, but he hardly makes us appreciate it, for again he is too vague and general:

> Ladies, this blind boy that ran from his mother,
> Will ever play the wag with one or other.

In Sidney's conclusion, on the other hand, Cupid's waggishness comes home to us because it is presented dramatically, and the poem ends on a very personal note with a wry smile:

> O how for joy he leapes, ô how he crowes,
> And straight therewith, like wags new got to play,
> Fals to shrewd turnes, and I was in his way.

This poem of Sidney's is no less worthy of attention because it is comic; in fact it is worthy of more serious attention than Greville's simply because it is a better poem, and it is the humorously dramatic presentation which makes it a better poem.

I suggest then that we should take Sidney seriously as a poet, but should always beware of taking him solemnly. Many occasions in our everyday life are at the same time serious and comic, and very many more occasions in Sidney's writings are. The description in the *New Arcadia* of Dorus struggling to write a verse-letter to Pamela is an instance:

. . . pen did never more quakingly performe his office; never was paper more double moistned with inke & teares; never words more slowly maried together, & never the *Muses* more tired, then now with changes & rechanges of his devises: fearing howe to ende, before he had resolved how to begin, mistrusting ech word, condemning eche sentence. This word was not significant, that word was too plain: this would not be côceived; the other would be il conceived. Here Sorow was not inough expressed; there he seemed too much for his owne sake to be sory. This sentence rather shewed art, then passion; that sentence rather foolishly passionate, then forcibly moving. At last, marring with mending, and putting out better, then he left, he made an end of it; & being ended, & diverse times ready to teare it: till his reason assuring him, the more he studied, the worse it grew, he folded it up, devoutly invoking good acceptation unto it. . . .[4]

4. Feuillerat, ed. cit., i, 356.

This is far from minimizing the seriousness to Dorus of what he is trying to do; but there is also a touch of absurdity in the situation as Sidney describes it, and Sidney's mockery of Dorus's efforts ('the more he studied, the worse it grew') is, after all, Sidney mocking his own poem,[5] while at the same time 'devoutly invoking good acceptation unto it. . . .'

5. Ibid., 357. A slightly different version of this poem, *O.A.* 74, is printed by Ringler, p. 122.

2

When I say *Stella*[1]

IT HAS BEEN ASSERTED THAT, in *Astrophil and Stella*, Sidney's passion is as real as Catullus';[2] and the assertion gives us, in a nutshell, one of the commonest approaches to the sequence. It demands that for 'Astrophil' we read 'Philip Sidney', for 'Stella' we read 'Penelope Rich née Devereux', and as the central fact of the poems we accept that Sidney was deeply in love with Penelope.[3] Apparently simple, this approach really raises more problems than it solves. It does not explain why the pseudonyms were used, it does not really account for the many sonnets which no one could describe as passionate (or, at least, it does nothing to encourage a proper appreciation of them), and—most unsatisfactory of all—it is derived from an unsubtle notion of the relation between a poet's life and his work. The reader who is so inclined may pick out from Sidney's sonnets those which seem most romantic (in both the literary and Hollywood senses of this word), decide that these express a 'real' passion of the 'real' Sidney, and then interpret the whole sequence in the light of this 'real' passion. In this way poems which apparently express this 'real' passion become the poet's real estate, and the rest of the sequence more or less inflated or debased currency. The comparison with Catullus has more point than was intended, since all we may think we know of his passion for Lesbia is drawn from some few of his poems.[4]

The approach I am criticizing makes insufficient allowance for that modification of a poet's own experience which is inevitable as it is translated into the public, conventional language and modes of

1. *A.S.* 28, Ringler, p. 179.
2. Wilson, *Sir Philip Sidney*, p. 203.
3. For facts known about Penelope see Ringler, pp. 440–6; Gentili, pp. 120–2, footnote.
4. Robert Rowland, intro. to *The Poems of Catullus*, with translations by James Michie, 1969, p. 12.

expression which he must use to express it. It is amusing to notice that, in one sonnet at least, Astrophil's experience is not merely as real as Catullus': partly at least, it *is* Catullus'. The poem addressed to Stella's sparrow, 'Good brother *Philip*, I have borne you long',[5] comes from 'Passer, deliciae meae puellae' and 'Lvgete, o Veneres Cupidinesque'.[6] It comes probably by way of Skelton,[7] which complicates the matter further. We cannot read this poem (can we read any poem?) as a simple transcript of personal experience. At the same time, and to be fair to those who read *Astrophil and Stella* as biography, it must be admitted that this very poem does something to encourage them. Addressing the sparrow by the name traditional for sparrows, Philip, Sidney is bound to remind us of himself. Indeed, the sparrow is *'brother Philip'*[8] in the first line, and even knighted ('sir *Phip*') in the last. Sidney demands that he himself be brought into the picture somewhere. The question is: where?

The temptation to seat him squarely in the centre of the canvas is certainly very great. In the *Apology*, for instance, he refers to his own poetry in this typically offhand way: 'Only, overmastered by some thoughts, I yielded an inky tribute unto them.'[9] This has been taken by some[1] as an account of the genesis of *Astrophil and Stella*. It has also been taken as expressing Sidney's concern over the state of English poetry at the time.[2] Each interpretation is as likely, or as unlikely, as the other: we simply do not know what 'thoughts' Sidney had in mind, or whether he had any particular ones in mind at all. That he means to sound nonchalant about his poetry is clear: any more precise interpretation is mere guesswork.

The sonnets have often been read as biography,[3] and Sidney's 'sincerity', at least in the 'better' ones, has often been stressed.[4] But to say that the poems succeed because Sidney is deeply moved and sincere,[4] or that the songs in the sequence are without doubt addressed to a real woman as we can easily tell from their tone,[5] is really to tell us nothing more than that Sidney has succeeded in giving that impression.

---

5. *A.S.* 83, Ringler, p. 208.   6. Catullus, ed. cit., Poems II and III, pp. 18, 20.
7. Ringler, p. 482.   8. My italics in *'brother'*.
9. Shepherd, p. 132.   1. Scott, op. cit., p. 22; Wallace, op. cit., p. 248.
2. Buxton, *Elizabethan Taste*, p. 278.
3. John, op. cit., p. 188; Wallace, op. cit., pp. 248–55; Mona Wilson, *Sir Philip Sidney*, pp. 167–204.
4. Pettet, op. cit., p. 232; Scott, op. cit., p. 53.   5. Scott, op. cit., p. 48.

The first sonnet, 'Loving in truth, and faine in verse my love to show',[6] which at a casual glance would seem to encourage a romantic reading, really shows its inadequacy. To read the poem as 'a manifesto of sincerity, an eloquent rejection of anything but the strictest devotion to honest feeling',[7] is to misread it. The 'rejection', we notice, is admitted to be 'eloquent', and eloquence, as all Renaissance writers knew, is bound to qualify 'honest feeling', whatever that may be. The skilful rhetoric in this poem has already been mentioned.[8] It is worth adding that this skill is displayed in a poem which is ostensibly about its writer's lack of skill; and the humour of that combination should not be missed:

> Thus great with child to speake, and helplesse in my throwes,
> Biting my trewand pen, beating my selfe for spite,
> 'Foole,' said my Muse to me, 'looke in thy heart and write.'

Far from being an advocacy of 'writing from the heart', the poem is both praise of Stella and a discussion of the best process for producing a poem.[9] To Sidney, as to all his contemporaries, the first stage in writing was *inventio*, or finding the subject matter, and one question discussed in this poem is whether the subject matter should be looked for in books or in the writer's mind. Astrophil decides in favour of the latter, which is what 'heart' means here.[1] As has been neatly pointed out,[2] if Astrophil had wanted to seek invention in the seat of his emotions, he would have had, in those days, to look in his liver. Apart from using an inadequate method, Astrophil made the mistake of working in the wrong order by seeking words (*elocutio*) before matter.[3] The inadequacy of such a comment on the poem as this is clear: 'This means that Sidney's love was sincere. . . .'[4]

Reading *Astrophil and Stella* as biography has at times been rather embarrassing to those who have done so. Mona Wilson writes: 'To me it is unthinkable that Sidney should have continued to address impassioned verse to Penelope Rich after he had made Frances Walsingham his wife.'[5] No doubt; but was it unthinkable to Sidney? We do not know, of course. We do know that Stella is represented in the sequence as a married woman and,

6. Ringler, p. 165. 7. Spencer, op. cit., pp. 268–9.
8. Above, p. 23. 9. Ringler, p. 458; Gentili, p. 217.
1. Ringler, p. 459. 2. Tuve, p. 39.
3. Ringler, p. 459. 4. Symonds, op. cit., p. 125.
5. *Sir Philip Sidney*, p. 202.

whatever trouble this caused Astrophil, it did not worry him because of any scruples over adultery: indeed, it is his failure to commit adultery which upsets him. Nevertheless, some readers have been upset by Astrophil's adulterous desires, or rather what they interpret as Sidney's adulterous desires. Grosart speaks morally, if not unkindly, on this subject[6] and proposes a re-ordering of the sonnets to clear Sidney's name:

... upon the dates of these Sonnets and Poems is contingent our verdict of shame or praise; and shame has been too readily pronounced. *E.g.* there are Sonnets that, though placed onward, seem to belong to a very early period, while 'Stella' in heart and hand was still free and to be wooed.[7]

Apart from its being in itself an unallowable procedure to tamper with the text in this way, it cannot even achieve its moral aim. Wherever they are placed, many poems can at their moral best only be interpreted as expressing the desire to fornicate:

> Let *Vertue* have that *Stella's* self; yet thus,
> That *Vertue* but that body grant to us.[8]

> But thou Desire, because thou wouldst have all,
> Now banisht art, but yet alas how shall?[9]

> Yet those lips so sweetly swelling,
> Do invite a stealing kisse:
> Now will I but venture this,
> Who will read must first learne spelling.

> Oh sweet kisse, but ah she is waking,
> Lowring beautie chastens me:
> Now will I away hence flee:
> Foole, more foole, for no more taking.[1]

Other poems, wherever they are placed, clearly express the desire to commit adultery:

> Is it not evill that such a Devill wants hornes?[2]

6. *The Complete Poems of Sir Philip Sidney*, 1873, I, xxxv–ix.
7. Ibid. xxxv. A footnote on p. xxxvi suggests some changes that might be made.
8. *A.S.* 52, Ringler, p. 191.   9 *A.S.* 72, ibid., p. 202.
1 *A.S.*, Song 2, ibid., p. 203.   2. *A.S.* 78, ibid., p. 206.

Symonds defends Sidney's character in a different way. He thinks Sidney can be excused to some extent because of the influence of his environment, one apparently in which people were all rather lax in sexual matters.[3] Symonds also suggests that Sidney would not have gone so far as he said he wanted to.[4] Stella, possibly bearing in mind the current low level of sexual morality, thinks it safer not to take the risk:

> Onely joy, now here you are,
> Fit to heare and ease my care:
> Let my whispering voyce obtaine,
> Sweete reward for sharpest paine:
> Take me to thee, and thee to me.
> 'No, no, no, no, my Deare, let be.'[5]

> 'Trust me while I thee deny,
> In my selfe the smart I try,
> Tyran honour doth thus use thee,
> *Stella's* selfe might not refuse thee.

> 'Therefore, Deere, this no more move,
> Least, though I leave not thy love,
> Which too deep in me is framed,
> I should blush when thou art named.'

> Therewithall away she went . . .[6]

She isn't too sure of herself, if it comes to that, which should have upset the Victorian moralists more.

A more recent writer, who rejects the obvious salve for such qualms—that it is Astrophil who wants to bed Stella and not necessarily Sidney Penelope—rejects it because he cannot see that it would make the situation more moral if the passion were only feigned.[7] But he does propose a salve, which, like Symonds's, is the result of his faith in his own insight into Sidney's mind:

To those literal-minded critics who talk of the sin of violating the sanctities of marriage he would have retorted by asking them to point out wherein the sanctity of the marriage of Lord and Lady Rich consisted.[8]

---

3. Symonds, op. cit., pp. 121-2.   4. Ibid.
5. *A.S.*, Song 4, Ringler, p. 210.   6. *A.S.*, Song 8, lines 98-101, ibid., pp. 220-1.
7. Wallace, op. cit., p. 255.   8. Ibid., p. 254.

That would have been a difficult question to answer, particularly if Sidney had been able to ask it two years after his own death when Lady Rich became the mistress of Sir Charles Blount, and if such a way of looking at marriage could be imagined of an Elizabethan.

Perhaps the strangest result of the attempts to read *Astrophil and Stella* biographically, and at the same time preserve as far as possible the notion of Sidney as a man of morals, is the addition to the text of two sonnets, 'Thou blind man's marke, thou foole's selfe chosen snare'[9] and 'Leave me ô Love, which reachest but to dust',[1] which do not belong there. This idea did not start with Grosart,[2] but his inclusion of the poems in his text of *Astrophil and Stella* as Sonnets 109 and 110[3] has had a great influence. He does attempt to justify his action on other than sentimental grounds, arguing that the word 'rich' in the third line of 'Leave me ô Love', 'Grow rich in that which never taketh rust', is a pun on Penelope's married name, and that the Latin motto which comes after the same poem, *Splendidis longum valedico nugis*, is meaningless unless the poem to which it refers forms part of *Astrophil and Stella*.[4] The first suggestion is an attractive one, because it is just what Sidney does do at times in the sequence itself.[5] The second suggestion is far less persuasive, since the sonnets and the motto may easily represent just a passing mood, or maybe an exercise in drama. However, neither argument carries any weight if we remember that the *Certain Sonnets*, the group of poems in which they occur, were probably written before *Astrophil and Stella*, and that there is no textual warrant for believing that Sidney intended them to be included in that sequence.[6]

Protests have been made against the assumption that these sonnets belong with *Astrophil and Stella*,[7] and Karl M. Murphy has dismissed the whole notion as absurd.[8] He is probably right in suggesting that the idea is tempting to the writer of a popular biography because it provides an easy way of rounding off an outline account of *Astrophil and Stella* and because it brings two of

---

9. *C.S.* 31, Ringler, p. 161.   1. *C.S.* 32, ibid.   2. Ibid., p. 423.
3. Grosart, ed. cit., pp. 71–2.   4. Ibid., p. 153.   5. See below, pp. 63–5.
6. Ringler, pp. 423–4.
7. Gerald Bullett, ed., *Silver Poets of the Sixteenth Century*, 1947, p. 418; Muir, *Introduction to Elizabethan Literature*, p. 43.
8. 'The 109th and 110th Sonnets of *Astrophel and Stella*', *P.Q.* xxxiv (1955), 349–52.

Sidney's best sonnets into discussion.[9] His suggestion that it is part of an 'attempt to fashion Sidney into the image of a Victorian gentleman'[1] is shrewd and makes a fair comment on remarks like that of L. C. John that Sidney in *Astrophil and Stella* is telling 'a story beginning with his realisation that he loved Stella too late and ending with his despair and final renunciation of earthly love'.[2] The fact that that remark was published in 1938 shows the persistence of the idea that Sidney must conform to Victorian moral standards.

It is not merely a matter of a mistake by Grosart; many have followed him either in regarding both sonnets as a conclusion to *Astrophil and Stella*,[3] or at least the second one, 'Leave me ô Love'.[4] There is a certain refinement in Wallace's notion that this poem was dissociated from the sequence to indicate some length of time in which the change in the lover's attitude could take place.[5] All the evidence from his poems, however, indicates that Sidney could think faster than that. Anyway, the suggestion is really an attempt to have it both ways. Wallace knows that these poems do not belong with *Astrophil and Stella*, but he thinks they should. And he thinks they should, like so many others, because he is not intent enough on catching Sidney's meaning in his poems, but is trying to force them into conformity with a meaning of his own.

None of this bother is necessary, of course, unless we make a complete and literal identification of Sidney with Astrophil and of Penelope with Stella, and also adopt a moral outlook which the poems never ask us to adopt. I have dwelt on the point not only because there is a frequent tendency to make this identification, but also because, although I think it is a mistake, this way of reading does answer to something in the poems themselves. It bears witness to Sidney's ability to involve the reader in the situa-

9. 'The 109th and 110th Sonnets of *Astrophel and Stella*', *P.Q.*, xxxiv (1955), p. 352.

1. Ibid.   2. John, op. cit., p. 55.

3. Ewald Flügel, ed., *Sir Philip Sidney's Astrophel and Stella und Defence of Poesie*, 1889, p. 62; J. B. Fletcher, 'Did "Astrophel" love "Stella"?' *M.P.* v (1907–8), 261; Mona Wilson, ed., *Astrophel and Stella*, p. xix; Winters, 'The Sixteenth Century Lyric in England', an essay in three parts, *P.C.* (February, March, April 1939), part iii, p. 39.

4. M. C. Bradbrook, *Shakespeare and Elizabethan Poetry: A Study of his Earlier Work in Relation to the Poetry of the Time*, 1964, p. 30; Lee, *Great Englishmen of the Sixteenth Century*, p. 114; Rees, op. cit., p. 61; L. B. Salomon, *The Devil Take Her! A Study of the Rebellious Lover in English Poetry*, 1961, pp. 83, 305.

5. Wallace, op. cit., p. 253.

tion he presents in *Astrophil and Stella* and, in a sense, make him believe in it. It bears witness also to the charm of Sidney's writings: some are so captivated by them that they feel impelled to defend their author even against himself.

However, reading the sequence as biography gives rise to more serious problems. Not only Sidney's morals have to be called into question, but even—at times—his artistic skill. I have already mentioned the sonnet which shows Stella as having a taste in pets suspiciously like that of Catullus' Lesbia.[6] This is but one instance of many of Sidney's use of conventional material. Stella looks remarkably like Petrarch's Laura, Astrophil's jealousy of Stella's dog[7] answers to Serafino's jealousy a century before, Astrophil's invocations to sleep,[8] dreams,[9] and his bed[1] were far from being the first invocations to sleep, dreams, and bed[2]—and so on. To the literal-minded reader, Sidney's imitativeness in many sonnets destroys their claim to be considered as biography.[3] This need worry us only if we think they make that claim.

It is particularly the early sonnets, the first thirty or so, which worry those in search of passionate personal experience. The sequence is then seen to liven up at the thirty-third sonnet,[4] if it is interpreted as an expression of Astrophil's anguish at having passed up a chance of marrying Stella. For the typically Victorian demand for sexual morality in poetry Dylan Thomas substitutes the typically modern demand for personal passion:

The sonnets are addressed to Penelope Devereux, whose father wished Sidney to marry her. They begin with elegance and pretence, poems moving like courtiers dressed in the habit of love. They are *about* love, they are not *in* love; they *address* love, they do not speak *out* of it. The raptures are almost easily come by; the despair almost as easily relinquished. They are the most perfect exercises for a man about to be in love. And Penelope married, and Sidney had lost her, and the sonnets were no longer rehearsals for a poetic event but poetry itself, striding and burning . . .[5]

6. See above, pp. 52–3.   7. *A.S.* 59, Ringler, p. 194.
8. *A.S.* 39, ibid., p. 184.   9. *A.S.* 32, ibid., p. 180.
1. *A.S.* 98, ibid., p. 230.
2. Lever, pp. 54–5, mentions these borrowings, but not in order to suggest that they detract from the value of Sidney's poems. Ringler's notes mention very many more borrowings.
3. Lee, *Elizabethan Sonnets, Newly Arranged and Indexed*, 1, xlii–xliii.
4. Ringler, p. 181.
5. 'Sir Philip Sidney', *Quite Early One Morning*, 1961, p. 119.

Thomas then quotes the thirty-third sonnet. This poem probably refers to Stella's marriage,[6] but it must be mentioned (not for the sake of saving Sidney's moral skin) that it could refer merely to a chance of meeting Stella which Astrophil had missed. The incident referred to may be either an important or a trivial one, then, and the interpretation we prefer will affect our reading of the poem considerably. If we think it refers to a missed meeting, then we may regard it as a hyperbolic expression of annoyance, rather than an expression of anguish, 'striding and burning'. Or we might even think that it reveals a stronger passion if Astrophil is so worked up at having merely missed a meeting. We might; but the point at issue here is not the power of this sonnet (which is un-doubted, whichever interpretation we take), but rather the quality of the previous thirty-two. I suggest that many of these are also very fine poems, if we do not look for 'raptures' which they do not necessarily pretend to offer.[7]

Why is the thirty-third sonnet open to such different interpreta-tions?

> I might, unhappie word, ô me, I might,
> And then would not, or could not see my blisse:
> Till now, wrapt in a most infernall night,
> I find how heav'nly day wretch I did misse . . .
> . . . I respects for both our sakes must show:
> And yet could not by rising Morne foresee
> > How faire a day was neare, ô punisht eyes,
> > That I had bene more foolish or more wise.[8]

If we think that this refers to something more serious than a missed meeting, we must take the phrases 'most infernall night', 'heav'nly day', 'by rising Morne', and 'How faire a day' as meta-phors:

. . . l'alba è il tempo in cui Stella aveva colpito Astrophil con la sua bellezza, senza però che lui arrivasse a riconoscere il proprio amore; il giorno è il compimento della felicità che Astrophil non è arrivato a cogliere, e la notte, la sua attuale situazione di rinuncia.[9]

It is quite reasonable to take the phrases that way. If we think the sonnet is about a meeting, then only 'infernall' and 'heav'nly' are

6. Ringler, p. 472, and Gentili, p. 293, are certain it does.

7. See above, pp. 3–6, for a discussion of one often criticized as merely conventional.

8. Ringler, p. 181.   9. Gentili, p. 293.

figurative,[1] which is also quite reasonable. Such problems of interpretation arise from the nature of language itself, and things are
always likely to become knotty when the language is that of poetry,
notoriously protean when we attempt to tie it down and demand a
simple answer.

If it is a marriage which is referred to, then we are brought right
back to Sidney and Penelope, since there were at one time nego-
tiations for their marriage.[2] Caution is still necessary, however.
The match with Penelope was only one of at least five which were
proposed for Sidney, so that its importance must not be exagger-
ated; and anyway for one in his position a love-match, except by
sheer coincidence, was out of the question.[3]

Faced with all these difficulties (or at least some of them, for the
attempt to justify Sidney morally need not be made), it is not
surprising that some scholars have swung to the other extreme
and suggested that *Astrophil and Stella* is pure (though, in one
sense of course, impure) fiction; but they have difficulty in mus-
tering sound arguments. J. M. Purcell emphasizes quite well the
deliberate artifice and customary lack of biographical intention in
Elizabethan poetry,[4] but pushes his point too far when he says:
'. . . if we judge by the sonnet tradition and by the professed
intentions and practices of Sidney's fellow sonneteers, *Astrophel
and Stella* cannot be accepted as autobiography.'[5] After all, Sidney
set the fashion for sonnet-sequences in England, and it would be
quite wrong to see his work as following in intention that of his
followers. The main fault with Purcell's book is his assumption
that poetry must be either 'a public declaration and the practice of
a poetical fashion' or 'the expression of an actual intimate relationship',[6] his failure to realize that it may be both. His arguments
against the evidence that some contemporaries identified Stella
with Penelope are feeble,[7] and they have been well answered.[8]
The one gleam of light in Purcell's book is his suggestion that

1. In 'by rising Morne' the word 'rising' is figurative, I suppose; but I doubt if
Sidney thought of it in that way, and even a modern reader is unlikely to do so.
2. Ringler, pp. 436–7.
3. D. E. Baughan, 'Sir Philip Sidney and the Matchmakers', *M.L.R.* xxxiii
(1938), 506–19.
4. *Sidney's Stella*, 1934, pp. 73–98.   5. Ibid., p. 98.   6. Ibid., p. 113.
7. Ibid., pp. 43–72.
8. H. H. Hudson, 'Penelope Devereux as Sidney's Stella', *H.L.B.*, no. 7 (April
1935), 89–129. The conclusion (on p. 128) is that 'informed people, from 1591
onwards, thought or knew that Penelope Devereux was Sidney's Stella . . .'

Sidney might well have addressed his poems to Penelope, who was a family friend, as a compliment.[9] This is, I think, a real possibility with some of the poems—the less passionate perhaps, and the particularly witty most likely—but Purcell never pursues the matter. And it needs pursuing. We might consider, for instance, just how far a writer in Sidney's circle of friends could go with sexual innuendo before a compliment became an insult.[1]

T. H. Banks seems to be on firmer ground when he stresses, quite rightly, that we cannot assume, because a poem moves us, that it springs from the poet's own experience and reflects his true character and his firm convictions.[2] Banks strengthens his case by referring to Sidney's assertions in his *Apology* that poetry is not tied down to facts as history is.[3] He also suggests a number of possible motives—the desire to express a Platonic affection, the desire to emulate the Italian poets, the desire to honour his country by his poetic achievement, and a sheer delight in artistic expression—any one of which would have been sufficient to impel Sidney to write.[4] True, but if we agree that Sidney's motives were probably mixed, that is hardly sufficient reason for denying the presence of yet another ingredient. Banks really falls down, as anyone arguing his case must, over the 'Rich' sonnets.[5] It is not true that these sonnets still make sufficient sense even though we think that no person called Rich is concerned in them, and that Penelope's marriage to Lord Rich is 'merely a coincidence that confuses the issue'.[6]

The evidence is too great for us to doubt that Sidney intends us, at least at times in his sequence, to identify Stella with Lady Rich.[7] A recent discovery by Jean Robertson is enough to dispel any doubts that might remain.[8] This is a manuscript of *The Manner of Sir Philip Sidney's Death* by George Gifford, Sidney's chaplain in his last days, which is apparently earlier than the one previously known, and which contains a short passage omitted from the later one:[9]

Hee added further I had this night a trouble in my mynde. For, examining my selfe, mee thought I had not a sure hold in Christ. After

9. *Sidney's Stella*, p. 97.   1. Discussed below, pp. 96–7, 133.

2. 'Sidney's *Astrophel and Stella* Reconsidered', *P.M.L.A.* l (1935), 404.

3. Ibid., 405.   4. Ibid., 409.   5. Discussed below, pp. 63–5.

6. Banks, op. cit., pp. 410–11.   7. Gentili, pp. 120–3.

8. Roger Howell, *Sir Philip Sidney, The Shepherd Knight*, 1968, p. 182.

9. Robertson, 'Sir Philip Sidney and Lady Penelope Rich', R.E.S., N.S. XV (1964), 296–7.

I had continued in this Perplexitie a while, Obserue how stranglie God did deliuer mee (For indeed it was a strange deliuerance that I had). There came to my remembrance a Vanitie wherein I had taken delight, whereof I had not ridd my selfe. It was my Ladie Rich. But I ridd my selfe of it, and presentlie my Ioy and Comfort returned within fewe howers.[1]

The other manuscript omits the words 'It was my Ladie Rich. But' and, although it could be argued that these words are a later insertion, this is unlikely because the manuscript which is without them lacks the cogency which they supply.[2] Even here, it should be noticed, the exact relationship between Sidney and Penelope is still left in doubt. To a fervent Christian *in extremis* almost anything might appear 'a Vanitie': we are not forced to conclude that there was a passionate love-affair.

It has been argued that it does not matter who Stella was, or even if she existed at all outside the poet's imagination.[3] But it does matter, and it is Sidney who makes it matter. If we take only a part of the evidence in the poems, those sonnets which play on the word 'rich', we are compelled to admit that Sidney is insisting on Stella's being identified with Lady Rich. The first time this word is played on, there is only a hint, although even here the mere repetition of the word makes the hint a rather broad one:

> Rich fooles there be, whose base and filthy hart
> Lies hatching still the goods wherein they flow . . .
> . . . that rich foole, who by blind Fortune's lot
> The richest gemme of Love and life enjoyes,
> And can with foule abuse such beauties blot;
> Let him, deprived of sweet but unfelt joyes,
> (Exil'd for ay from those high treasures, which
> He knowes not) grow in only follie rich.[4]

The next instance is not so insistent but is more explicit:

> . . . now long needy Fame
> Doth even grow rich, naming my *Stella's* name.[5]

1. Ibid., 297.   2. Ibid.   3. Bullett, ed. cit., p. xiv.
4. *A.S.* 24, Ringler, pp. 176–7.
5. *A.S.* 35, ibid., p. 182. Some texts have 'meaning' instead of 'naming', and W. G. Friedrich, in 'The Stella of Astrophel', *E.L.H.* iii (1936), 114–39, where he argues that Stella is not Lady Rich, says (p. 129): 'The context clearly shows that the word "meaning" is not used in the modern sense, but in the sense of "declaring",

Sonnet 37 must be quoted in full:

> My mouth doth water, and my breast doth swell,
>> My tongue doth itch, my thoughts in labour be:
>> Listen then Lordings with good eare to me,
> For of my life I must a riddle tell.
> Towardes *Aurora's* Court a Nymph doth dwell,
>> Rich in all beauties which man's eye can see:
>> Beauties so farre from reach of words, that we
> Abase her praise, saying she doth excell:
> Rich in the treasure of deserv'd renowne,
> Rich in the riches of a royall hart,
> Rich in those gifts which give th'eternall crowne;
> Who though most rich in these and everie part,
>> Which make the patents of true worldly blisse,
>> Hath no misfortune, but that Rich she is.[6]

Even if 'of my life' is a mere exclamation used to fill out the line, there can be no doubt that this sonnet refers to Lady Rich.[7] Six uses of the word 'rich' (with the additional possibility of laying a meaningful stress on the word 'reach' in the seventh line, a stress which would suit the tone of the poem) leave no doubt that the answer to the riddle must lie in the meaning that we give to 'Rich' in the last line.[8] To find why it is her misfortune for Stella to be married and 'Rich' we need to study the sequence as a whole, and particularly the twenty-fourth sonnet[9] (which it is quite natural to turn to since it also plays on this word) and the seventy-eighth.[1] Finally, in the seventy-ninth sonnet[2] a kiss is described in this way:

> A double key, which opens to the heart,
> Most rich, when most his riches it impart . . .

Most obviously, 'his riches' means the riches of the heart; but may there not also be the meaning of the riches which belong to Lord

6. *A.S.* 37, Ringler, p. 183.

7. Jack Stillinger, 'The Biographical Problem of *Astrophel and Stella*', *J.E.G.P.* lix (1960), 625–6.

8. The use of a capital letter here, which suggests a proper name, is not confined to one early text; see Ringler, p. 473.

9. Ibid., p. 176.   1. Ibid., p. 205.   2. Ibid., p. 206.

"setting forth".' But see Ringler, p. 472, and especially Gentili, p. 300: 'La lezione di 1–2, *meaning my* Stellas *name*, sottolinea con ancor maggiore evidenza l'allusione . . .'

Rich, the jealous husband mentioned in the sonnet immediately before?

The more or less cryptic nature of these references gives some support to the idea that *Astrophil and Stella* could have been read in two distinct ways: as biography by those in Sidney's circle and therefore in the know, or as a piece of fiction by those outside this circle.[3] Spenser in *Astrophel*,[4] an elegy on Sidney dedicated to his widow, assumes that Stella is to be identified with her. Spenser seems to have been outside the inner circle of Sidney's friends, and so this rather comic identification may simply be the result of Spenser's ignorance. On the other hand, it is more likely, I think, that Spenser who, like most of his contemporaries,[5] did not attach as much importance to the biographical interpretation of poetry as we are inclined to, was simply creating the myth he thought most suitable to the occasion.[6]

Some play may be made of the fact that the first edition of *Astrophil and Stella* was seriously incomplete. The main omissions are Sonnet 37[7] (in which the punning on Lady Rich's name is most obvious), the eleventh song[8] (an intimate conversation at night between Astrophil and Stella at her window), lines 69–100 of the eighth song[9] (where Stella reveals her love for Astrophil), and lines 25–42 of the tenth song[1] (lines which spoil the obvious conclusion to be drawn from these omissions by being no more revealing of intimacies between the two than many passages included in this edition). These omissions may be the result of there being two manuscripts of *Astrophil and Stella* in circulation, one for intimate friends, and one (less revealing) for the wide world outside.[2] This involves believing that Sidney had two distinct audiences in mind, which would correspond roughly to those since Sidney's day who have read the sequence as biography and those who have read it as a piece of conventional writing.[3] Unfortunately

---

3. Hamilton, 'The Modern Study of Renaissance English Literature: A Critical Survey', *M.L.Q.* xxvi (1965), 176–7.

4. Spenser, p. 546.

5. Lewis, *English Literature in the Sixteenth Century*, 322.

6. Buxton, *Sir Philip Sidney and the English Renaissance*, pp. 216–17, and *Elizabethan Taste*, p. 281.

7. Ringler, p. 183.   8. Ibid., p. 233.   9. Ibid., p. 220.   1. Ibid., pp. 226–7.

2. Buxton, *Sir Philip Sidney and the English Renaissance*, p. 184, and *Elizabethan Taste*, pp. 270–1. Scott, op. cit., p. 22, and Wallace, op. cit., p. 249, also believe the passages were omitted to avoid scandal.

3. See Howe, op cit., p. 150, for a list of them.

for the theory, even without these passages there is still enough to satisfy a gossip-columnist.[4] Moreover, the text of this edition is corrupt, and consequently not a firm basis for such an argument: the ten songs included in it are published as a group at the end of the sonnet-sequence, there are several odd lines omitted for no apparent reason, and many of its words are wrong.[5]

The theory of two distinct audiences ignores one of the salient facts which any reading of *Astrophil and Stella* should take account of—its continual movement between fact and fiction. True, an awareness of this is only possible for someone who knows at least some details of the author's life and character; but in Sidney's day as in our own there would be few readers who did not. *Astrophil and Stella* often refers to at least three real people, Sidney himself and the Riches, but it would be a mistake to insist on always taking what it says literally and historically, and—to complicate matters still further—it would be unfair to divide the sonnets into those which are 'sincere' and those which are mere 'literary exercises'.[6] The terms themselves are too loose for us to do this: we can know nothing of a writer's 'sincerity', except what we infer from his poems, so that to talk of it is only another (and a worse) way of saying that we think a poem is successful; and every poem is, after all, in some sense a 'literary exercise'.

F. S. Boas suggests a way out: 'While . . . the *Astrophel and Stella* cycle has its basis in the true and moving story of Philip Sidney and Penelope Devereux, it probably admitted an element of dramatic fantasy.'[7] This approach lends itself to a subtlety of reading, in keeping with the subtlety of Sidney's writing, which the purely biographical and purely fictional approaches do not. For instance, the early sonnets, so often thought to be too conventional, may have their conventionality justified as a dramatic device. Sidney

may have wished to show how Astrophel—who should not be completely identified with the poet—progressed from a conventional love to a genuine passion. Shakespeare similarly distinguished Romeo's speeches about Rosaline with his speeches to Juliet.[8]

4. Stillinger, op. cit., 620.   5 Ringler, p. 542.

6. Lewis, *English Literature in the Sixteenth Century*, p. 328: '. . . we must not listen at all to critics who present us with the preposterous alternative of "sincerity" (by which they mean autobiography) and "literary exercise".'

7. Boas, op. cit., p. 153. See also Muir, *Introduction to Elizabethan Literature*, p. 42.

8. Muir, *Introduction to Elizabethan Literature*, pp. 46–7; Muir, *Sir Philip Sidney*, p. 30.

This is very persuasive; my doubts about it come from my belief that many of the best poems in the sequence occur early on, and need no dramatic justification for their existence if we are not seeking 'passion', while the dullest poems are to be found late on in the sequence.[9]

Is it fair to suggest that to think of the sequence as carefully planned is 'to credit Sidney with a dramatic art beyond the compass of his age'?[1] The word 'age' is ambiguous here. If what is meant is the time in which Sidney lived, then we recall the flowering of the drama so soon after his death. The seeds were there in his lifetime (*Tamburlaine* and *The Spanish Tragedy* were produced only a couple of years after his death), even though this may not have been apparent then.[2] If what is meant is Sidney's youth, then the argument has even less weight. It is unfair to say that he was too young to have dramatic ability, and so deny the evidence of it in his work. The evidence of it must be looked for in his work, and there it can be found. My main objection to reading *Astrophil and Stella* as basically expressing a real passion, with the admixture of dramatic elements, is simply that it does not credit him with enough dramatic power.

The question of how far *Astrophil and Stella* is conceived dramatically is very important, for our understanding of the sequence as a whole, and also for our interpretation of many of the details in it.

> . . . ev'n of fellowship, ô Moone, tell me
> Is constant *Love* deem'd there but want of wit?
> Are Beauties there as proud as here they be?
> Do they above love to be lov'd, and yet
> > Those Lovers scorne whom that *Love* doth possesse?
> Do they call *Vertue* there ungratefulnesse?[3]

The last line there has worried a lot of people. Three interpretations have been proposed. The least persuasive, I think, is the suggestion that '*Vertue*' means something like 'constancy in love', and Astrophil is asking if this is found unpleasing.[4] It is true that

9. e.g., Sonnets 86, 89, 94, 95, 96, Ringler, pp. 212, 223, 228, 229.
1. Mona Wilson, *Sir Philip Sidney*, p. 203.
2. Sidney was not hopeful for the drama in England; see Shepherd, pp. 133–7.
3. *A.S.* 31, Ringler, p. 180.
4. C. R. B. Combellack, 'Sidney's *With how sad steps, o Moon*', *Explicator*, xx, no. 3 (1961–2), Article 25; Kalstone, p. 164.

'ungratefulnesse' could take this sense then; but I do not think that '*Vertue*' means anything like 'constancy in love'.[5] Moreover, this reading gives a very weak sense, all the more disappointing since, in its context, the line comes out like a slap across the face.

A better interpretation is that which seems to have been suggested first by Lamb: 'The last line of this poem is a little obscured by transposition. He means, Do they call ungratefulness there a virtue?'[6] This interpretation is accepted by many,[7] and the discovery of several possible sources in Italian[8] strengthens the case for it. However, Sidney was not bound to follow the sense of his sources, and this interpretation still leaves the line considerably marred,[9] not just 'a little obscured', by a transposition for which no other reason can be suggested than sheer incompetence on Sidney's part. True, he often disturbs the normal prose-order of his words, but never to such an extent. The inversion in this line: 'Where ys Ah that face, that a Sunne defaces?'[1] which makes the line ambiguous, is as bad an example of inversion as Sidney can show elsewhere; and it is not as contorted as the line I am discussing would be if Lamb were right.

The best interpretation is this:

. . . in the sestet Sidney asks four questions. The first is aimed at those who regard his constancy as foolish; the next two are aimed at Stella who, he implies, is the conventional proud beauty who despises the lover she deliberately attracts; and the last is aimed at himself for stigmatizing Stella's virtue, or chastity, as ingratitude.[2]

This interpretation has several advantages: the meaning given to '*Vertue*' is clearly acceptable; it avoids a clumsy inversion which renders the line almost impossible to read aloud intelligibly;[3] and

5. I think it means 'chastity' here. For a discussion of the use of the word 'virtue' in *A.S.*, see below, pp. 74–6.

6. 'Some Sonnets of Sir Philip Sidney,' *The Prose Works of Charles Lamb*, 1835, iii, 141.

7. C. S. Burhans, 'Sidney's *With how sad steps, o Moon*', *Explicator*, xviii, no. 4 (1959–60), Article 26; E. H. Essig, 'Sidney's *With how sad steps, o Moon*', ibid. xx, no. 3 (1961–2), Article 25; Ringler, p. 472; Gentili, p. 290; Poirier, ed. and trans., *Sir Philip Sidney: Astrophel and Stella*, p. 77.

8. C. W. Lemmi, 'Italian Borrowings in Sidney', *M.L.N.* xlii (1927), 77–9.

9. Robertson, 'Sir Philip Sidney and his Poetry', *Elizabethan Poetry*, p. 126.

1. *C.S.* 5, Ringler, p. 138.

2. Muir, *Sir Philip Sidney*, p. 29.

3. Muir, ' "Astrophel and Stella", XXXI', *N.Q.*, n.s. vii (1960), 51, and review of Ringler, 232.

the sudden reversal of meaning in the sonnet, by which Astrophil turns on himself, is in tune with many others in the sequence.[4] There is nothing against this reading except the shock which it gives to an over-serious or romantic reader; and such a reader must either get used to shocks or give up Sidney for another poet.

This sort of thing happens again and again in *Astrophil and Stella*. For instance, a sonnet[5] may begin with Astrophil apparently annoyed by his enslavement to Stella:

> What, have I thus betrayed my libertie?
> Can those blacke beames such burning markes engrave
> In my free side? or am I borne a slave,
> Whose necke becomes such yoke of tyranny?

and apparently determined to throw off the yoke:

> Vertue awake, Beautie but beautie is,
> I may, I must, I can, I will, I do
> Leave following that, which it is gaine to misse . . .

only for him to sink under her spell again at the end of the sonnet:

> O me, that eye
> Doth make my heart give to my tongue the lie.

That ending comes as a shock, certainly; but then it is realized that it was inevitable: the tone of

> Vertue awake, Beautie but beautie is,
> I may, I must, I can, I will, I do . . .

is at odds with what is said, for Astrophil's determination has something comically desperate about it.[6] Similarly, the irony of Astrophil's turning on himself in the last line of Sonnet 31: 'Do they call *Vertue* there ungratefulnesse?' has been prepared for: the moon climbing the skies—with 'sad steps' and 'how wanne a face'

4. Muir, 'Astrophel and Stella', 52. The ones suggested are Sonnets 2, 5, 21, 30, 33, 47, 71, 72, with nos. 5 and 21 particularly relevant.
5. *A.S.* 47, Ringler, p. 188.
6. Rudenstine, p. 179, calls it a 'near-comic call to arms'.

like the conventional Elizabethan lover and like Astrophil of course—cuts a figure not only pitiful, but also absurd.[7]

What might seem to be a comparatively minor matter, then— a disagreement over the interpretation of one line—is really related to our approach to the whole sequence, whose dramatic qualities as a whole are mirrored in little in many of the individual sonnets.

If the sonnets are as dramatic, both individually and collectively, as I suggest, then there will be real dangers of misreading if we try to trace a consistent 'philosophy' in them. Nevertheless, the attempt is sometimes made. J. A. Symonds, worried by the fact that they were written for a married woman, seeks some compensation for this in what he calls 'their purity of tone and philosophical elevation of thought'.[8] This need not delay us, except for one moment to wonder whether we are thinking of the same poems; it is in fact merely another attempt to excuse Sidney's morals, and

> castum esse decet pium poetam
> ipsum, uersiculos nihil necesse est.[9]

Astrophil is hardly a philosophical person: he is neither a lover of wisdom intent on expressing the general causes and principles of things, nor one who accepts suffering with calm resignation. Admittedly, he does at times play with philosophical ideas:

> True, that true Beautie Vertue is indeed,
> Whereof this Beautie can be but a shade,
> Which elements with mortall mixture breed:
> True, that on earth we are but pilgrims made,
>   And should in soule up to our countrey move:
> True, and yet true that I must *Stella* love.[1]

He plays here with the platonic notions that the Beautiful and the Good are the same, and that physical beauty is only a 'shade' of the Idea of the Beautiful,[2] and with the Christian notion that on earth we are but pilgrims to a heavenly city, only in order to deny their value to him since he is in love with physical beauty itself in the shape of Stella. He is using platonic and Christian ideas tactically,[3] just as at times he assumes a Petrarchan mask;[4] he is not really

7. Muir, *Sir Philip Sidney*, p. 29.   8. Symonds, op. cit., p. 116.
9. Catullus, ed. cit., Poem XVI, p. 42.   1. *A.S.* 5, Ringler, p. 167.
2. Ibid., p. 461.   3. Poirier, *Sir Philip Sidney*, pp. 186–9.
4. Hamilton, 'Et in Arcadia Ego', *M.L.Q.* xxvii (1966), 348.

much concerned with the idea of love; his concern is with his own
psychology rather than with metaphysics.[5]

Astrophil is reluctant to generalize, except momentarily as one
stage in a process which is always empirical; ideas, like other
experiences of his, are used, but always as a way of expressing his
particular circumstances and his love for Stella.[6] He says:

> I beg no subject to use eloquence,
> Nor in hid wayes to guide Philosophie:
> Looke at my hands for no such quintessence;
> But know that I in pure simplicitie,
>   Breathe out the flames which burne within my heart,
>   *Love* onely reading unto me this art.[7]

We must of course be careful how literally we take this: Astrophil
may not be writing in order 'to use eloquence', but he *is* using
eloquence, nevertheless, and the 'pure simplicitie' in which he
breathes out flames is an 'art'. All the same, the insistence that
Stella is a real woman, not merely an idea,[8] and the effect of the
sonnet as a whole, which is to show us the importance of this real
woman to Astrophil, are typical of the sequence. And so, inciden-
tally, is the faint comic suggestion that Astrophil is a fire-breathing
dragon.

The search for some philosophical 'quintessence', some abstract
framework on which the sequence is arranged, or some generalized conclusions which Astrophil comes to in the course of the
sequence, is bound, I think, to distort the effect of the poems. It is,
like the purely biographical and purely fictional approaches, understandable as an attempt to see this complicated, and often con-
tradictory, set of poems as a whole; but it is ill advised.

This is very easily seen, I think, if we consider the suggestion
that the love expressed in *Astrophil and Stella* is a platonic manner
of loving, moving from earthly to heavenly beauty.[9] This argument depends very much on the acceptance of 'Thou blind man's
marke' and 'Leave me ô Love'[1] as the last two sonnets of the
sequence,[2] which they are not:[3] 'The two sonnets at once round

5. Lever, p. 71; de Mourgues, op. cit., p. 16, on Sonnet 60.
6. Gentili, pp. 149–50.   7. *A.S.* 28, Ringler, p. 179.
8. See above, p. 40.   9. Fletcher, op. cit., pp. 256–7.
1. *C.S.* 31 and 32, Ringler, p. 161.   2. Fletcher, op. cit., p. 261.
3. See above, pp. 57–8.

up the dramatic sequence by the triumph of Stella, the star of love, seen first as Woman, then as God, and epitomize the platonic principle of evolution at its highest.'[4] Stella is nowhere seen as God, of course;[5] the god, if any god, who dominates *Astrophil and Stella* is Cupid, playful and changeable, whimsical and dramatic in what he does. The sequence ends inconclusively with Astrophil still both pleased and annoyed with Stella and with his love for her:

> So strangely (alas) thy works in me prevaile,
> That in my woes for thee thou art my joy,
> And in my joyes for thee my only annoy.[6]

There have been other attempts to read the sequence as basically philosophical, and better ones. R. L. Montgomery sees the sonnets as, despite their wit and playfulness, basically serious,[7] and as mainly concerned—beneath their Petrarchan motifs and a few circumstantial details—with 'a persistent struggle between Astrophel's rational and passionate impulses, and his meditative self-exploration'.[8] That 'thematic dimension'[9] is certainly there. So is this one:

Astrophel, the lover, is critical, above all, of the modes of public allegiance to a religion of love, though he has no private mode to substitute effectively for it and though he must adopt its conventions often to express his devotion.[1]

Even this is arguably correct:

By the end of the sequence, through his relation to Stella, Astrophel has been made aware of the nature of Love as the Petrarchan universal: he has discovered himself as part of the convention, which, by virtue of his participation in it, has acquired permanent validity.[2]

My objection to these theories is not that they are untrue—indeed, I think they are all true, and they are certainly well argued

4. Fletcher, op. cit., p. 262.

5. It is said that she 'shrines in flesh . . . a Deitie' in *A.S.* 4; but the indefinite article is important, and so is the humorous context. See p. 76 below.

6. *A.S.* 108, Ringler, p. 237.

7. 'Reason, Passion, and Introspection in *Astrophel and Stella*', 129.

8. Ibid., p. 127.   9. Ibid.

1. David Kalstone, 'Sir Philip Sidney and "Poore *Petrarchs* long deceased woes" ', *J.E.G.P.* lxiii (1964), 32.

2. Young, p. 88.

—but simply that they are only part of the truth. Their very solemnity is so out of keeping with the wit and lightness of touch which run through the sequence as to be positively misleading. They simply do not answer to our experience of reading *Astrophil and Stella*. Its delicate and subtle wit is not simply the sugar on a philosophical pill; it is so pervasive as to demand to be an essential part of any response.

> The wisest scholler of the wight most wise
> By *Phoebus'* doome, with sugred sentence sayes,
> That Vertue, if it once met with our eyes,
> Strange flames of *Love* it in our soules would raise . . .[3]

Astrophil is here using an idea mentioned also in the *Apology*:[4] '. . . if the saying of Plato and Tully be true, that who could see virtue would be wonderfully ravished with the love of her beauty . . .'[5] But he is using the idea with more than a hint of mockery, as we can see from the play on 'wisest' and 'most wise' and the alliteration on 'w' in the first line, and the obtrusive alliteration again in 'with sugred sentence sayes'. He is also, in the use of the word 'flames', apparently harmless enough at this point, preparing for a further twist.[6] The poem ends:

> Vertue of late, with vertuous care to ster
> Love of her selfe, takes *Stella's* shape, that she
> To mortall eyes might sweetly shine in her.
> It is most true, for since I her did see,
>   Vertue's great beautie in that face I prove,
>   And find th'effect, for I do burne in love.

'Vertue' has by this time, we see, revealed herself as all too humanly and comically anxious to be loved and working hard to make sure that she is. Astrophil's love, as the word 'burne' makes clear, is sexual passion, an interesting comment on the 'Strange flames' which 'Vertue' was said to be able to raise, in fact the opposite of the platonic love mentioned in the beginning of the poem. Moreover, if we take 'It is most true' in the twelfth line as referring to all the preceding part of the poem,[7] then an invalid argument is used: if we could see virtue, we would love it; I love

3. *A.S.* 25, Ringler, p. 177.   4. Ibid., p. 469.
5. Shepherd, p. 119.   6. Kalstone, p. 154.
7. But see Ringler, p. 469.

Stella; therefore Stella is an embodiment of virtue. Astrophil knows that this is an invalid argument, and so the poem as a whole is comic.

What comes out of that poem, which is typical, is our sense of the working of Astrophil's mind in love. The ideas in the poem are to be taken seriously only in the sense that they help to build up a good poem (and a good poem is a worthwhile thing) and in so far as they tell us something more of the complex character of Astrophil and something more of his complex predicament. It is no more reasonable to work out ideas of general validity from this sonnet, than it is to argue that the one which follows it proves that Sidney was a believer in astrology.[8] 'Though dustie wits dare scorne Astrologie'[9] contains two arguments. The first is that great causes (in this case the stars) must give great effects. This seems reasonable enough (its converse is, after all, used in a traditional proof for the existence of a personal God: since we have personality, we could not have been caused by something without personality, something lesser than ourselves); but Astrophil's second argument is so deliberately fanciful and anti-climactic as to make mockery of the first, particularly since it is said to be more powerful than the first:

> And if these rules did faile, proofe makes me sure,
> Who oft fore-judge my after-following race,
> By only those two starres in *Stella's* face.

Astrophil does not really care about astrology, only about Stella.

More important, to my mind, than trying to draw general philosophical conclusions from the sonnets is making sure that we understand correctly the terms which they use. Only if we understand these terms correctly can we appreciate the witty play Astrophil makes with them. As an important instance—Astrophil is often concerned with the claims of 'virtue' as against those of love. When used of Stella this word means 'chastity':[1]

> O thinke I then, what paradise of joy
> It is, so faire a Vertue to enjoy.[2]

Astrophil does not intend to follow Stella's advice and take pleasure in being chaste himself as she is chaste: he wants to 'enjoy', in the sexual sense, her chastity.

8. As does Craig, op. cit., p. 34.   9. *A.S.* 26, Ringler, p. 177.
1. See also above, p. 68.   2. *A.S.* 68, Ringler, p. 200.

That is a simple and obvious meaning of 'virtue'; but the word has a different meaning when applied to a man. The tension which Astrophil often feels between virtue and love has nothing to do with a horror of adultery.[3] Astrophil struggles with his passion because it hinders the predominance of reason in him, and it turns his life aside from the course he thinks it should take.[4] Without going so far as to agree that this refusal to recognize physical love as properly one of the major preoccupations of life, this fear of letting oneself be turned aside from what are considered to be higher ends, is 'un trait permanent du caractère national',[5] we must admit its importance to Sidney and his contemporaries. Virtue, in a man, as many of the sonnets make plain,[6] is to be understood in something approaching the sense of the Latin *virtus*, manliness. This is the sense it has in the *New Arcadia* when Zelmane is challenging Anaxius: '. . . but even in thine owne vertue (whereof thou so much gloriest) I will make my triall . . .'[7] and later, when Zelmane is fighting Anaxius: '. . . in all the combats that ever she had fought, she had never more need of quicke senses, & ready vertue'.[8] Love is a danger because it may distract the lover from more manly pursuits, as Spenser's Prince Arthur says:

> That idle name of loue, and louers life,
> As losse of time, and vertues enimy
> I euer scornd . . .[9]

This acquiescence in 'losse of time' is precisely the fault of Spenser's Verdant in the Bower of Bliss:

> His warlike armes, the idle instruments
> Of sleeping praise, were hong vpon a tree,
> And his braue shield, full of old moniments,
> Was fowly ra'st, that none the signes might see;
> Ne for them, ne for honour cared hee,

---

3. Howell, op. cit., p. 183. See also above, p. 55.
4. Poirier, ed. and trans., *Sir Philip Sidney: Astrophel and Stella*, pp. 26–7.
5. Poirier, *Sir Philip Sidney*, p. 182.
6. e.g., *A.S.* 18, 21, 64, Ringler, pp. 173, 175, 198.
7. Feuillerat, ed. cit., i, 505.
8. Ibid., 516. Zelmane is not fighting for 'her' chastity: 'she' is really Pyrocles.
9. *F.Q.*, 1.ix.10, Spenser, p. 46.

Ne ought, that did to his aduauncement tend,
But in lewd loues, and wastfull luxuree,
His dayes, his goods, his bodie he did spend:
O horrible enchantment, that him so did blend.[1]

That may be compared with this:

Your words my friend (right healthfull caustiks) blame
My young mind marde, whom *Love* doth windlas so,
That mine owne writings like bad servants show
My wits, quicke in vaine thoughts, in vertue lame:
That *Plato* I read for nought, but if he tame
Such coltish gyres, that to my birth I owe
Nobler desires, least else that friendly foe,
Great expectation, weare a traine of shame.[2]

In other words, love hinders him in his career; 'vertue' connotes worldly success, glory, making one's mark in the world; it has little to do with Christian ideas of sexual morality.

Virtue is seen as an eminently reasonable thing, and so to accuse virtue of attempting to usurp reason (placed on the side of love) makes another instance of Astrophil's sense of humour:

Vertue alas, now let me take some rest . . .
But if that needs thou wilt usurping be,
The litle reason that is left in me,
And still th'effect of thy persuasions prove:
I sweare, my heart such one shall shew to thee,
That shrines in flesh so true a Deitie,
That *Vertue*, thou thy selfe shalt be in love.[3]

This is similar to the occasion when reason, having argued at first against love, is stricken with Stella's eyes, and

Reason thou kneel'dst, and offeredst straight to prove
By reason good, good reason her to love.[4]

Shrewd psychological insight, and the humorously dramatic way in which it is presented (itself part of the insight) is what strikes us here.

1. *F.Q.* ii.xii.80, ibid., p. 139.   2. *A.S.* 21, Ringler, p. 175.
3. *A.S.* 4, ibid., pp. 166-7.   4. *A.S.* 10, ibid., p. 170.

I see Astrophil, then, as a dramatic character, in the sense that he likes to dramatize himself and his feelings, and also in the sense that he should not necessarily, or lightly, be identified with his creator. I regard as inadequate these approaches: the purely biographical (or at least that which sees the sequence as aspiring primarily to biography), which does not allow sufficiently for the conventional and dramatic elements which are undoubtedly present; the purely fictional, which ignores the biographical elements; the approach which regards the sequence as based on Sidney's personal experience but including some elements of drama, fiction, and convention, because even this (a more fruitful approach than any of the others, I think) still seems to me to lay too much stress on a passionate love-affair which we can know of only from the sequence itself; and the thematic approach, because it necessitates a straitjacket (or rather, several straitjackets, for several themes have been suggested) out of which the poems are always madly and gaily bursting.

However, like anyone who suggests an approach to the sequence as a whole, I am in danger of being hoist with my own petard—a fate and an image which would, I am sure, have appealed to the witty and military-minded Sidney and to his creation, Astrophil, who had similar interests.[5] How does my approach differ from the purely fictional? Is it not open to the same objection? For instance, I have just been discussing Astrophil's dramatic play with the idea of virtue. Now, it is evident from several sonnets that Astrophil feels the claims of this virtue strongly:

> . . . since mad March great promise made of me,
> If now the May of my yeares much decline,
> What can be hoped my harvest time will be?[6]

Does not this lead us straight back to Sidney and the claims of the biographical approach? Greville remembers Sidney in his youth: 'His talk ever of knowledge, and his very play tending to enrich his mind . . .'[7] Greville says again:

. . . the truth is: his end was not writing, even while he wrote; nor his knowledge moulded for tables, or schooles; but both his wit, and understanding bent upon his heart, to make himself and others, not in words or opinion, but in life, and action, good and great.[8]

5. *A.S.* 2, ibid., p. 165.
6. *A.S.* 21, ibid., p. 175; see also, e.g., *A.S.* 18, ibid., p. 173.
7. Greville, op. cit., p. 6.   8. Ibid., p. 18.

And Astrophil is like Sidney in many ways: he is aware of current
political problems,[9] he takes part in tournaments,[1] he is very well
read in the French and Italian poets, and so on. At times, even,
Astrophil must be identified completely with Sidney. They have
the same father, Sir Henry Sidney, three times Lord Deputy of
Ireland, anyway:

> . . . How *Ulster* likes of that same golden bit,
> Wherewith my father once made it half tame . . .[2]

If, then, I suggest an approach which stresses first and foremost
the dramatic nature of the sequence, I must square this with the
frequent appearance of the real Sidney, and the real Penelope Rich,
on the stage.

We return, almost, to where we started in this chapter. It is not
surprising that so many readers take these poems as biography.
Again and again in them we sense the day-to-day life, the actual
circumstances, surrounding Astrophil and Stella,[3] and even the
world of international politics.[4] This is why the biographical
approach, although ultimately inadequate, satisfies so many: there
is biography in the sequence. The problems are to recognize it
when it occurs, not to see it when it does not occur, and above all,
to understand the part it plays in the drama.[5] But even the most
outrageous, the most moralizing, biographical approach shows,
I think, a better appreciation of the effect which Sidney creates
than, for instance, does a futile search for rhyme-links in the
sonnets,[6] or an emphasis on their rhyme-schemes.[7]

Lamb's famous comment may be criticized on details; but it is
not famous for nothing:

. . . they are not rich in words only, in vague and unlocalised feelings—
the failing too much of some poetry of the present day—they are full,
material, circumstantiated. Time and place appropriates every one of

9. See, e.g., *A.S.* 30, Ringler, p. 179.   1. *A.S.* 41, 53, ibid., pp. 185, 191.
2. *A.S.* 30, ibid., p. 180. The 'golden bit' was a land-tax which Sir Henry enforced
to provide support for his troops (ibid., p. 471).
3. F. T. Prince, 'The Sonnet from Wyatt to Shakespeare', *Elizabethan Poetry*
(Stratford-upon-Avon Studies 2), p. 19.
4. Muir, *Sir Philip Sidney*, pp. 32–3.   5. See below, pp. 84–95.
6. J. M. Bullitt, 'The Use of Rhyme Link in the Sonnets of Sidney, Drayton, and
Spenser', *J.E.G.P.* xlix (1950), 14–32.
7. R. G. Whigam and O. F. Emerson, 'Sonnet Structure in Sidney's "Astrophel
and Stella" ', *S.P.* xviii (1921), 347–52.

them. It is not a fever of passion wasting itself upon a thin diet of dainty words, but a transcendent passion pervading and illuminating action, pursuits, studies, feats of arms, the opinions of contemporaries and his judgment of them. An historical thread runs through them, which almost affixes a date to them; marks the *when* and *where* they were written.[8]

I think Lamb over-emphasizes the passion; and there is much virtue in his 'almost', because it is extremely difficult to fix the dates when they were composed;[9] and we can only *think* we know where they were composed, and then only if we take them more literally than perhaps we should.[1] Nevertheless, Lamb is right about the effect which the poems make: when reading them we do think of a real man in a real time and place. That we do so is partly a triumph of dramatic art, and partly a result of the fact that there *are* real people in them. If the phrase be not taken too literally (a discourtesy I do not intend), these poems answer perfectly to Marianne Moore's definition of what poems should be: they are 'imaginary gardens with real toads in them . . .'[2]

8. Lamb, op. cit., p. 149.   9. Ringler, pp. 435–40.
1. e.g., *A.S.* 84, ibid., p. 209.   2. 'Poetry', *Collected Poems*, 1951, p. 41.

3

This Theater of pleasure[1]

IT IS, OF COURSE, possible to recognize that the presentation of *Astrophil and Stella* is in many ways dramatic—the interplay of its numerous characters is a main feature, and we are continually overhearing soliloquies and lively conversations[2]—without conceding that it is basically a dramatic *fiction*.

The manner in which the sequence was first presented to the public is important. Nashe's preface to this first edition may easily be ignored or treated rather slightingly, because it is so obviously an extended blurb: 'Put out your rush candles, you Poets and Rimers, and bequeath your crazed quaterzayns to the Chaundlers; for loe, here he cometh that hath broke your legs.'[3] Yet even a blurb may contain some good criticism, and I think this one does. Nashe's dominant metaphor is a theatrical one, and this is shrewd, even if he does present it rather too theatrically: '. . . so endes the Sceane of Idiots, and enter *Astrophel* in pompe.'[4] He calls the sequence 'this Theater of pleasure'[5] and 'a paper stage streud with pearle',[6] and even suggests what kind of play is being performed: '. . . the tragicommody of loue is performed by starlight.'[7] He also gives the best brief summary of the action which I know of: 'The argument cruell chastitie, the Prologue hope, the Epilogue dispaire . . .'[8]

Now, I think this approach by a contemporary of Sidney, and a man of real poetic ability himself, should not be dismissed too lightly. Perhaps we should not give too much credit to Nashe for realizing that the publication of *Astrophil and Stella* was an epoch-making event in the history of English poetry—this is the sort of

1. Thomas Nashe, 'Somewhat to read for them that list', a preface to *Astrophel and Stella* (first Newman edition of 1591), *Elizabethan Critical Essays*, ed. G. Gregory Smith, 1904, ii, 223.

2. Ringler, p. xliv.	3. Nashe, op. cit., p. 225.	4. Ibid., p. 223.	5. Ibid.
6. Ibid.	7. Ibid.	8. Ibid.	

thing blurb-writers often say, and every century or so one of them is liable to be right by accident—but Nashe says much more than that. He recognizes that elaborate ornamentation is an important feature of Sidney's style here even if, which Nashe does not mention, Astrophil often disclaims it while he uses it:

> Some one his song in *Jove*, and *Jove's* strange tales attires,
> Broadred with buls and swans, powdred with golden raine:
> Another humbler wit to shepheard's pipe retires,
> Yet hiding royall bloud full oft in rurall vaine . . .
> I can speake what I feele, and feele as much as they,
> But thinke that all the Map of my state I display,
> When trembling voice brings forth that I do *Stella* love.[9]

Nashe rejoices in this elaborate eloquence; in fact, the dominant note of his preface is one of excitement and pleasure. Moreover, the reader is invited to enjoy the drama for itself: he is not asked to welcome the autobiography of Sir Philip Sidney. Nashe nowhere speaks of Sidney directly and, although Nashe was presumably outside the inner circle of Sidney's friends, he could hardly have been unaware of Sidney's fame which five years before had been sealed by a spectacular death. Nashe, an Elizabethan, does not make what is often nowadays the automatic attempt to relate the poet's work immediately to the poet. He delights, and expects others to delight, in the skill with which the poems were written.

Nashe's description of the drama as a 'tragicommody of loue'[1] is quite an accurate one.[2] Perhaps he is thinking partly of the fact that no one dies at the end, and perhaps partly of the fact that comedy usually involved fictitious characters, unlike tragedy;[3] but above all it strikes me as a felicitous term for a work which, while its matter is often in itself sadness and frustration, nevertheless displays such frequent wit, good humour, and sheer comedy. Nashe remembers, what Sidney also knew and demonstrated so often, that 'Sonets be not bound prentise to annoy':[4] even when 'annoy' is the subject matter, they are made to give pleasure.

---

9. *A.S.* 6, Ringler, pp. 167–8.   1. Nashe, op. cit., p. 223.
2. Gentili, p. 154. See also ibid., pp. 150–1, for a justification of Nashe's presenting *Astrophil and Stella* metaphorically as a stage-play.
3. Evans, op. cit., p. 100, mentions this distinction.
4. *A.S.* 70, Ringler, p. 201.

The very use of the names 'Astrophil' and 'Stella' indicates how Sidney wished his work to be taken.[5] He obviously could have written in his own person if he had wanted to; he could easily have related the poems directly to himself and Penelope. Both the names he uses are descriptive, of course, and that fact alone is some justification for their use: 'Stella' is descriptive of beauty and inaccessibility, and 'Astrophil' of feelings towards Stella. It is true, too, that the last syllable of 'Astrophil' contains a hint of Sidney himself. All the same, the effect of using these pseudonyms, and of keeping allusions to real people indirect and occasional, is to help make the sequence primarily a dramatic fiction.

What Sidney's feelings were towards Penelope we do not know; nor, as readers of poetry, do we need to know. I am, in arguing that we should regard *Astrophil and Stella* primarily as a dramatic fiction, not saying that there was nothing between Sidney and Penelope; I am not saying anything about their relationship except what the poems themselves suggest that we should consider. Simply, it seems to me the most fruitful approach, and the one most in accord with the poems, to take them in the way they are presented to us, which seems in all essentials to match what Sidney would have wished. My concentration, then, is on what was produced and not on the way in which it might have been produced.

I have not mentioned before one possibility which is by itself sufficient to upset many approaches to the sequence: we cannot be sure that all these poems were addressed originally to the same person,[6] we cannot be sure that they were all addressed to anyone at all (except, of course, the reader whom all poetry implies), and we cannot be sure that they were all originally intended to form part of the one large work. None of this matters,[7] if we take the poems as they stand and relate them only to such people and events outside themselves as they require, and only when they require. The poems do not exist, they were not written, to provide the historian with facts about Sidney's life. What is important is that sometimes the poems bring to our notice known facts of

---

5. Buxton, *Sir Philip Sidney and the English Renaissance*, p. 105.

6. Stillinger, op. cit., pp. 626–8.

7. I am not suggesting that it would not matter if, for instance, more biographical allusions in the poems were identified.

Sidney's life, which then become relevant to the poems because they are part of them.[8]

To suggest that we regard the poems primarily as fiction is not to imply that they therefore matter less than they would do as biography. We naturally take plays and novels as fiction, unless and only when we have good reason for doing otherwise. There is a difference, of course, with lyric poetry, which is so often subjective in a more obvious way than are plays and novels; and *Astrophil and Stella* is made up of lyric poems. It is not merely a random collection, however: the total is greater than the sum of its parts, and the total is presented in a way that suggests it is 'feigned', and, we remember, 'the feigned may be tuned to the highest key of passion',[9] or of humour, or of wit, or of poetry.

The distinction between Astrophil and Sidney has been expressed in a way that I think is not acceptable. It is not correct to suggest that Astrophil is blunt and plain-spoken, while Sidney is skilful and ingenious.[1] The argument here is that Astrophil must eschew literary skill if he is to appear sincere to Stella, while Sidney must have this literary skill in order to write the poems.[2] Both these arguments are correct, as far as they go; but in the sequence Astrophil is represented as writing poems in which he uses literary skill and ornament while disclaiming them. A poem may begin with a disclaimer; Astrophil will not speak like other lovers, and he mocks their way of speaking:

> Some Lovers speake when they their Muses entertaine,
> Of hopes begot by feare, of wot not what desires:
> Of force of heav'nly beames, infusing hellish paine:
> Of living deaths, deare wounds, faire stormes and
>   freesing fires . . .[3]

and finish with Astrophil insisting on his own simple sincerity:

> I can speake what I feele, and feele as much as they,
> But thinke that all the Map of my state I display,
> When trembling voice brings forth that I do *Stella* love.[4]

But, in order to account for the glaring fact that these poems do not tremble, but are rather vigorous and forceful, we need not

---

8. Buxton, *Elizabethan Taste*, pp. 271–2.   9. Shepherd, p. 110.
1. Buxton, review of Montgomery, *R.E.S.*, n.s. xiv (1963), 100.
2. Buxton, *Elizabethan Taste*, pp. 278–9.   3. *A.S.* 6, Ringler, p. 167.
4. Ibid., p. 168.

postulate 'some mythical or lost love poems behind the ones we are reading',[5] poems written by Astrophil and not by Sidney, plain blunt poems by a plain blunt man. This poem itself contains both the plainness at the end and the elaboration at the beginning, and also a further elaboration which is the relationship between these two. The distinction between artless Astrophil and artful Sidney is an over-simplification,[6] simply because in the sequence it is Astrophil who attacks ornateness, apparently to impress Stella with his artlessness,[7] Astrophil who uses artifice while disclaiming it. What I am saying is not a version of the old argument that Macbeth is a poet because he speaks in fine blank verse: Macbeth is not represented as a literary man, and Astrophil is.

A similar distinction seems to me to be also misleading. It is not fair to suggest that for the lady addressed in the poems there is plain simplicity, and for other readers 'all the similitudes and decoration that the emotion will maintain'.[8] Stella is nowhere represented as stupid. She must appreciate as much as anyone the paradox of these poems, the paradox of all poetry, that artifice leads to reality.

The comparison sometimes made between Sidney and Herbert in this respect is useful if we see also an essential difference between them. Herbert often adopts the pose of a simple man:[9]

> Who sayes that fictions onely and false hair
> Become a verse? Is there in truth no beautie?
> Is all good structure in a winding stair?
> May no lines passe, except they do their dutie
>   Not to a true, but painted chair? . . .
>
> Shepherds are honest people; let them sing:
> Riddle who list, for me, and pull for Prime:
> I envie no mans nightingale or spring;
> Nor let them punish me with losse of rime,
>   Who plainly say, *My God, My King.*[1]

5. Hallett Smith, *Elizabethan Poetry: A Study in Conventions, Meaning and Expression*, 1952, p. 151. The suggestion is made with reference to *A.S.* 6.

6. J. P. Castley, '*Astrophel and Stella*—"High Sidnaean Love" or Courtly Compliment?' *M.C.R.*, no. 5 (1962), 55: 'This *is* an over-simplification, because most of the time Astrophel is very consciously using art, playing a part.'

7. Montgomery, p. 72.　　　8. Hallett Smith, *Elizabethan Poetry*, p. 152.

9. Martz, op. cit., pp. 269–71.

1. '*Jordan* (I)', *The Works of George Herbert*, ed. F. E. Hutchinson, 1941, pp. 56–7; see also '*Jordan* (II)', ibid., p. 102.

The resemblance to so many poems in *Astrophil and Stella* is clear: Herbert has obviously said much more than '*My God, My King*'. The difference, however, is important. Herbert is disclaiming ingenuity in his own person, while in *Astrophil and Stella* it is Astrophil, the dramatic character, who disclaims it. There is in this way, then, a kind of complication in Sidney's sequence which is not in Herbert's poems. Sidney's poems are placed at a further remove from their author, and only occasionally is the *persona* who speaks them merged with the author, occasionally and in varying degrees.[2]

Sometimes what we may call the biographical intrusion is fairly obvious and definite, as in the mention of 'my father' with details which make it clear that it is Sidney's father who is referred to,[3] or the 'Rich' sonnets that identify Stella with Penelope Rich.[4] Sometimes the biographical intrusion is not only less obvious, but also less definitely there: we can only say that the lines seem to suggest Sir Philip Sidney himself. When Astrophil mentions 'that friendly foe,/Great expectation',[5] and says 'mad March great promise made of me',[6] we may think of Sidney, and of the great hopes people had of him; but we cannot be sure that we are intended to. Again, when we see Astrophil taking part in tournaments,[7] we cannot be sure that we should bring Sidney himself to mind. Perhaps we are on firmer ground when the sonnets echo Sidney's other works. An image used in the *Apology*, '. . . it was found that the astronomer looking to the stars might fall into a ditch . . .'[8] is used also in *Astrophil and Stella*:

> For though she passe all things, yet what is all
> That unto me, who fare like him that both
> Lookes to the skies, and in a ditch doth fall?[9]

The image is admittedly a commonplace,[1] but against that we notice that the poem in which it occurs is again one in which Astrophil is bewailing his failure to fulfil his early promise:

> O let me prop my mind, yet in his growth
> And not in Nature for best fruits unfit . . .[2]

2. Hamilton, 'Et in Arcadia Ego', 349.
3. *A.S.* 30, Ringler, p. 180; quoted above, p. 78.
4. See above, pp. 63–5.   5. *A.S.* 21, Ringler, p. 175.
6. Ibid.   7. *A.S.* 41 and 53, ibid., pp. 185, 191.
8. Shepherd, p. 104.   9. *A.S.* 19, Ringler, p. 174.
1. Shepherd, p. 167.   2. *A.S.* 19, Ringler, p. 174.

We cannot be sure, but we feel there is intended to be a hint of Sidney. On the other hand, it would probably be stretching a point to suggest that the love of horsemanship which is obvious in the *Apology*[3] should make us think of Sidney every time Astrophil mentions horses or uses equine imagery.[4] Then there are hints which are more or less broad according to the reader. The heraldic allusions would certainly be noticed more easily by readers in Sidney's day than by readers now, but it is doubtful if everyone then would have caught them:

> *Cupid* then smiles, for on his crest there lies
> *Stella's* faire haire, her face he makes his shield,
> Where roses gueuls are borne in silver field.[5]

It is possible to take that simply as an ornate description of Stella's face—the red cheeks which are always attractive, on a background of that extreme pallor which the Elizabethans at least found attractive; but there is also an allusion to the Devereux arms—*argent, a fesse gules, in chief three torteaux*,[6] in other words silver or white, with a red band across the middle, and three red discs at the top. Similarly, Astrophil's arms bear a close resemblance to Sidney's which were *or, a pheon azure*[7] (a blue arrow-head on a gold background); speaking to Cupid, Astrophil says:

> Yet let this thought thy Tygrish courage passe:
> That I perhaps am somewhat kinne to thee;
> Since in thine armes, if learnd fame truth hath spread,
> Thou bear'st the arrow, I the arrow head.[8]

There is also an earlier allusion to Sidney's arms:

> It is most true, what we call *Cupid's* dart,
> An image is, which for ourselves we carve . . .[9]

This is by no means as certain an allusion as the first one I mentioned, but I think it must be considered likely when we think of it in connection with the first, which can hardly be doubted, and also with another:

> *Vertue's* gold now must head my *Cupid's* dart.[1]

3. Shepherd, p. 95.
4. See above, pp. 32–3, and below, p. 116.
5. *A.S.* 13, Ringler, p. 171.
6. Ibid., p. 465.   7. Ibid., p. 479.
8. *A.S.* 65, ibid., p. 198.
9. *A.S.* 5, ibid., p. 167. See W. H. Bond, 'Sidney and Cupid's Dart', *M.L.N.* lxiii (1948), 258.   1. *A.S.* 72, Ringler, p. 202.

Since, traditionally, Cupid's golden arrows caused love, while his leaden ones caused the rejection of love, and Sidney has changed the significance of the golden arrows drastically,[2] we are probably intended to remember that gold is an heraldic tincture and so catch an heraldic allusion here; we notice that it is '*my Cupid's* dart'.[3]

The biographical intrusion, then, works by hints and sometimes guesses; but its recurrence makes it strangely, even mystifyingly, insistent. It adds an extra depth, and also an enigmatic quality, to any poem in which it occurs. When, for instance, Astrophil warns Stella's sparrow against too much boldness with her, he is probably warning Philip Sidney also,[4] as well as himself (the last syllable of his name is the same as the first syllable of the sparrow's):

> Good brother *Philip*, I have borne you long . . .
> Leave that sir *Phip*, least off your necke be wroong.[5]

What exactly Sidney might be warned to stop doing we can only guess. It may be something to do with Penelope in so far as she is sometimes identified with Stella, and perhaps he is being warned against making this very identification; but we cannot be sure. There are similar mysteries any time there is biographical intrusion. What we need is some way of describing the general effects which this always has, for I think it is done for deliberate and important artistic effects which are quite precise, even though in particular instances there are other subtleties too.

In *Astrophil and Stella* it is Sidney who is glimpsed at moments behind Astrophil, and not the other way about. In other words, the biographical intrusion is not meant as a form of personal confession, but rather as a way of adding another character to the drama. Similarly, Penelope Rich is glimpsed at moments behind Stella; and the way that the main 'Rich' sonnet[6] opens on the world of historical fact is dramatic:[7] the fact becomes an element of the fiction, and gives a sort of solidity to the drama.[8] The sudden references to reality have the effect of making us more aware of the fiction, more conscious that the sequence is mainly fiction.[9] Awareness of the author, and of his guiding hand in the affair, increases our appreciation of the sequence as a made thing, an

2. Ibid., p. 480. 3. My italics on '*my*'.
4. Buxton, *Elizabethan Taste*, p. 290; Young, p. 70.
5. *A.S.* 83, Ringler, p. 208. 6. *A.S.* 37, ibid., p. 183.
7. Young, p. 22. 8. Ibid., p. 38.
9. Gentili, p. 166.

artefact, something that did not merely happen, and consequently increases our delight in the skill the poems reveal.

This is not all that happens, however. Sidney is quite fond of building up a poem in an elaborately conventional way, and then suddenly causing a kind of reality to interrupt the convention. His poem about the nightingale shows this:[1]

> The Nightingale, as soone as Aprill bringeth
> Unto her rested sense a perfect waking,
> While late bare earth, proud of new clothing springeth,
> Sings out her woes, a thorne her song-booke making . . .
>
> Alas she hath no other cause of anguish
> But *Thereus'* love, on her by strong hand wrokne,
> Wherein she suffring all her spirits' languish,
> Full womanlike complaines her will was brokne.
>   But I who dayly craving,
>   Cannot have to content me,
>   Have more cause to lament me,
> Since wanting is more woe then too much having.
>   O *Philomela* faire, ô take some gladnesse . . .[2]

The witty line 'Since wanting is more woe then too much having' and the phrase 'Full womanlike' interrupt the convention in which the poem is set, and so make us not only more conscious of the fact that it is set in a convention, but also more conscious of the fact that the convention has a relation to reality. Paradoxically, such interruptions, by making us more aware of a poem as art, make us more aware too that art is connected with the world outside it. The same technique is at work in 'The ladd *Philisides*':

> So I unlucky lad
> Whome hills from her do hemme,
> What fitts me now but teares, and sighings sadd?
> O fortune too too badd,
> I rather would my sheepe
> Thad'st killed with a stroke,
> Burnt *Caban*, lost my cloke,
> Then want one hower those eyes which my joyes keepe.
> Oh! what doth wailing winne?
> Speeche without ende were better not begin.[3]

1. Discussed above, pp. 1–2. See also Thompson, *The Founding of English Metre*, p. 155.
2. *C.S.* 4, Ringler, p. 137.   3. *O.P.* 5, lines 95–104, ibid., p. 259.

The line 'Burnt *Caban*, lost my cloke', humorous by the triviality of the disasters it mentions against the solemnity of the lament as a whole, and humorous too in its suggestion of a real shepherd with mundane worries in contrast to the literary conventional shepherd who is Philisides, by disrupting the convention both makes us more aware of its existence and more aware that it does relate to reality. The name 'Philisides' has the same meaning as 'Astrophil', and it suggests Philip Sidney even more strongly than does 'Astrophil', which intensifies the effect I have described.

This is, then, as I see it, the chief reason for the biographical intrusions into the dramatic fiction which is *Astrophil and Stella*: to make us more aware of the poetry as art, and consequently more aware that art is related to things outside itself. I believe the effect is deliberately calculated by Sidney. He was as aware as anyone can be of the paradoxical nature of art. Artistry is needed when we wish to appear natural,[4] since poetry is always made by a human being,

> The only creature ever made who fakes,
> With no more nature in his loving smile
> Than in his theories of the natural style . . .[5]

There is also the paradox that subject-matter which is painful in itself becomes pleasant in art:

> Oft cruell fights well pictured forth do please.[6]

This is reminiscent of the *Apology*:

> That imitation whereof Poetry is, hath the most conveniency to Nature of all other, insomuch that, as Aristotle saith, those things which in themselves are horrible, as cruel battles, unnatural monsters, are made in poetical imitation delightful.[7]

His *Apology* shows too how seriously he took fiction, and how aware he was that fiction, by its very difference from some kinds of fact, bears a closer relation to others.[8]

4. Shepherd, p. 138: Tully 'would have his words (as it were) double out of his mouth, and so do that artificially which we see men do in choler naturally'.
5. Auden, ' "The Truest Poetry is the most Feigning" ', *Collected Shorter Poems 1927–1957*, 1966, p. 317.
6. *A.S.* 34, Ringler, p. 181.
7. Shepherd, p. 114. See also the quotation from *O.A.* 13, p. 35, above.
8. Shepherd, pp. 102–3.

Some comparisons may help to make clearer what I think Sidney is doing, and perhaps strengthen my argument that he is doing it deliberately. Sidney's occasional intrusion of himself, and other historical characters like Penelope and Lord Rich and Sidney's father, into his dramatic fiction is not dissimilar to Spenser's intrusion of himself into the last complete book of the *Faerie Queene*. Spenser appears first in the pastoral disguise of 'Colin Clout', which makes the identification clear to those who have read other poems of Spenser, particularly *Colin Clouts Come Home Againe*,[9] but still, like Sidney's biographical intrusions, not too blatant. It is perhaps significant that the incident is the one in which Sir Calidore interrupts the dance of the Graces around the girl to whom Colin Clout is piping, a dance which may be interpreted as a vision of harmony in the world in general and the harmony of art in particular:

> She was to weete that iolly Shepheards lasse,
> > Which piped there vnto that merry rout,
> > That iolly shepheard, which there piped, was
> > Poore *Colin Clout* (who knowes not *Colin Clout*?)
> > He pypt apace, whilest they him daunst about.
> > Pype iolly shepheard, pype thou now apace
> > Vnto thy loue, that made thee low to lout:
> > Thy loue is present there with thee in place,
> Thy loue is there aduaunst to be another Grace.

> Much wondred *Calidore* at this straunge sight,
> > Whose like before his eye had neuer seene,
> > And standing long astonished in spright,
> > And rapt with pleasaunce, wist not what to weene;
> > Whether it were the traine of beauties Queene,
> > Or Nymphes, or Faeries, or enchaunted show,
> > With which his eyes mote haue deluded beene.
> > Therefore resoluing, what it was, to know,
> Out of the wood he rose, and toward them did go.

> But soone as he appeared to their vew,
> > They vanisht all away out of his sight,
> > And clean were gone, which way he neuer knew;

9. Spenser, p. 535.

All saue the shepheard, who for fell despight
Of that displeasure, broke his bag-pipe quight,
And made great mone for that vnhappy turne . . .[1]

The vision of harmony is interrupted not only by Sir Calidore but, in so far as it is a microcosm of the artistic world of the *Faerie Queene*, an elaborately wrought fiction, interrupted also by the suggestion of the appearance of the author himself. Then, at the end of the last canto of this last book, Spenser appears without any disguise, so breaking off the spell which the whole work has laid upon us, and simultaneously reminding us of the fictional, artistic nature of the work and of its close relation to the reality outside it. The effect here is shocking and dramatically appropriate. Spenser is speaking at first, of course, of the Blatant Beast's having broken from captivity:

So now he raungeth through the world againe,
    And rageth sore in each degree and state;
    Ne any is, that may him now restraine,
    He growen is so great and strong of late,
    Barking and biting all that him doe bate,
    Albe they worthy blame, or cleare of crime:
    Ne spareth he most learned wits to rate,
    Ne spareth he the gentle Poets rime,
But rends without regard of person or of time.

Ne may this homely verse, of many meanest,
    Hope to escape his venemous despite,
    More then my former writs, all were they cleanest
    From blamefull blot, and free from all that wite,
    With which some wicked tongues did it backebite,
    And bring into a mighty Peres displeasure,
    That neuer so deserued to endite.
    Therefore do you my rimes keep better measure,
And seeke to please, that now is counted wisemens
        threasure.[2]

1. *F.Q.* vi.x.16–18, ibid., p. 381. To appreciate the effect fully we need to read at least the whole of this canto.
2. *F.Q.* vi.xii.40–1, ibid., p. 393. I have, in the second stanza, substituted 'cleanest' for 'clearest'; see *The Works of Edmund Spenser: A Variorum Edition*, ed. Edwin Greenlaw, C. G. Osgood, F. M. Padelford, Ray Heffner (general editors), and J. G. McManaway, D. E. Mason, Brents Stirling, 1961, vi, 467.

The *Faerie Queene* is an allegory, of course, while *Astrophil and Stella* is only occasionally allegorical;[3] but the difference is not important for my purpose here. If allegory, so often spoken of as though complete consistency of allegory were the ideal, although an impossible ideal,[4] does not require this consistency always, indeed may benefit from the occasional disruption of the allegory, so also may poems not allegorical, particularly when the poems are written by one so insistent that

therein (namely in moral doctrine, the chief of all knowledges) he [the poet] doth not only far pass the historian, but, for instructing, is well nigh comparable to the philosopher, and, for moving, leaves him behind him . . .[5]

There is an interesting crux in the *Pilgrim's Progress*, which is also relevant. The book's opening is well known:

As I walked through the wilderness of this world, I lighted on a certain place, where was a den; and I laid me down in   *The gaol* that place to sleep: and as I slept I dreamed a dream. I dreamed, and behold I saw a man clothed with rags . . .[6]

The 'den', with its gloss '*The gaol*', is a clear reminder of Bunyan himself just before the dream moves us away from him into the realm of allegory, of fiction. The crux comes much later on: '. . . I awoke from my dream. And I slept and dreamed again . . .'[7] The question of why Bunyan allows himself to awake and then makes himself fall asleep again has caused some bother.[8] A good artistic reason for this can be found.[9] We may ask ourselves why Bunyan bothers to mention the dream at all. It was a traditional way of opening a fantasy, of course; but he need not have insisted on it to such an extent: on page after page we find remarks like 'So I saw in my dream'[1] and 'Then I saw in my dream'.[2] I think Bunyan does this to remind us that his book is a piece of fiction,

3. See above, pp. 33, 38–42.
4. Rosemary Freeman, *Edmund Spenser*, 1962, p. 26.
5. Shepherd, p. 120.
6. John Bunyan, *The Pilgrim's Progress*, ed. Roger Sharrock, 1965, p. 39.
7. Ibid., p. 162.
8. H. A. Talon, *John Bunyan*, 1964, p. 17.
9. An artistic reason, different from the one I suggest but not in conflict with it, is proposed in J. F. Forrest, 'Bunyan's Ignorance and the Flatterer: A Study in the Literary Art of Damnation', *S.P.* lx (1963), 14–15.
1. Bunyan, op. cit., p. 41.   2. Ibid., p. 124.

not to be taken literally, and simultaneously, by stressing the fiction in contrast to the reminders of the historical John Bunyan, to remind us of the relation of the fiction to a reality outside itself. The awakening and falling asleep again make the same effect, only rather more strongly. There is something similar in the Valley of the Shadow of Death:

> . . . ever and anon the flame and smoke would come out in such abundance, with sparks and hideous noises (things that cared not for Christian's sword, as did Apollyon before) that he was forced to put up his sword, and betake himself to another weapon called All-Prayer: so he cried in my hearing, '*O Lord I beseech thee deliver my Soul.*'[3]

We move from the allegorical sword, through the trite metaphor of 'weapon', to the strictly literal 'All-Prayer', and the allegory is deliberately interrupted. I cannot believe that Bunyan's imagination was unable to cope allegorically with 'the flame and smoke'; no, just as an appreciation of a single metaphor or simile depends on our being simultaneously aware of both similarity and difference (difference because, if there were no difference, there would be nothing interesting in the similarity), so allegory, or indeed any fiction, depends on our realizing that it is both different from the world outside it and also very like it. It is interesting to notice that, when Christian prayed, he 'cried in my hearing'—another of Bunyan's biographical intrusions.

Returning to *Astrophil and Stella*, after this intrusion of comparisons, we may see a special interest in Song 8. This is the last stanza:

> Therewithall away she went,
> Leaving him so passion rent,
> With what she had done and spoken,
> That therewith my song is broken.[4]

With the contrast between 'him' and 'my' we move from Astrophil to Philip Sidney.[5] Why is this so striking? I suggest that it is because we have here biographical intrusion with the effects I have described. The song is particularly far removed from the personal and immediate, being in the third person and in the past tense, so that the sudden shock of 'That therewith my song is broken' brings us down to earth and the present and the real Sidney who

3. Ibid., p. 97.   4. Lines 101–14, Ringler, p. 221.
5. Buxton, *Elizabethan Taste*, p. 292.

has written the poem: the poem as artefact is strengthened by this movement, and so is our sense of its relation to reality. Similarly, one mention of Sidney's arms occurs in a poem very much concerned at first with the obviously fictional, indeed allegorical, Cupid:

> . . . when, nak'd boy, thou couldst no harbour find
> In this old world, growne now so too too wise:
> I lodg'd thee in my heart, and being blind
> By Nature borne, I gave to thee mine eyes.[6]

The conventionality and fictional nature of those lines are highlighted, and their relation to reality is suggested, by these lines:

> . . . I perhaps am somewhat kinne to thee;
> Since in thine armes, if learnd fame truth hath spread,
> Thou bear'st the arrow, I the arrow head.[7]

At 'Thou bear'st the arrow' we are still in the most conventional of literary worlds; but 'I the arrow head' reverberates with relevance to Sidney himself.[8]

What the precise relevance is in this instance we cannot be sure, any more than we can be sure that all such biographical intrusions have yet been noticed. I doubt very much whether the first readers of the poems among Sidney's friends were sure, just as I doubt that all of them would catch all of the hints of Sidney himself in his poems. Did they, for instance, see an allusion to Penelope's married name here?

> The doore by which sometimes comes forth her Grace,
> Red Porphir is, which locke of pearle makes sure:
> Whose porches rich (which name of cheekes endure)
> Marble mixt red and white do enterlace.[9]

My guess is that Penelope, and anyone else who may have read the poem when it was first written, would have been left wondering, and that they were intended to be left wondering. How we take each biographical intrusion as it occurs, indeed even sometimes whether we think one does occur, depends in each instance on what we think the manner and intention of the poem are. I do think, however, that all the definite biographical intrusions have the dominant effects which I have described.

6. *A.S.* 65, Ringler, p. 198.   7. Ibid.   8. See above, pp. 86–7.
9. *A.S.* 9, Ringler, p. 169. This poem is discussed above, pp. 3–6.

Probably the poems teased, and to some extent mystified, the first readers among Sidney's friends, just as they tease and mystify us now. Readers are bound to disagree often as to how seriously to take many lines of Sidney. We may wonder, for instance, about the sudden parenthesis in this passage:

'Graunt, ô graunt, but speech alas,
Failes me, fearing on to passe,
Graunt, ô me, what am I saying,
But no fault there is in praying.

'Graunt, ô deere, on knees I pray,
(Knees on ground he then did stay)
That not I, but since I love you,
Time and place for me may move you. . . .'[1]

There is here no biographical intrusion into Astrophil's desperate plea to Stella;[2] but the sudden comment in the third person (rather like a stage-direction), coming as from outside Astrophil's situation, has the effect of making us see him from another angle, a humorous angle. This does not, I think, destroy the seriousness of his plight, but rather helps us to see that it has its ridiculous as well as its serious side. The effect is not so different from that of the biographical intrusions which both emphasize that the poems are skilful artefacts and hint at their relation to the raw material of art, the poet's life and experience.

Astrophil and Stella, and the suggestions of Sidney and Penelope which sometimes hover behind them, are far from making up the whole of the cast of the drama. There are many other characters, presented with varying degrees of force and solidity: Stella's husband, whose failure to appreciate his wife's virtues is a foil to Astrophil's adoration of her; various friends of Astrophil, usually addressed with real or assumed annoyance since they never appreciate his state of mind; other ladies, who try their best but cannot match up to Stella; the Muse, sometimes invoked, and the Muses, often scorned; Cupid, with whom Astrophil has a complicated love–hate relationship; and various personifications struggling in Astrophil's mind.

1. *A.S.*, Song 8, lines 45–52, Ringler, p. 219. I have included a comma after 'me' in line 46, a correction suggested by Jack Stillinger, review of Ringler, *J.E.G.P.* lxii (1963), 375.
2. There is at the end of the poem, however; see above, p. 93.

Stella's husband is seen in the role of the conventional obstacle to the lover's enjoyment of his love:

> *Astrophil* with *Stella* sweete,
> Did for mutuall comfort meete,
> Both within themselves oppressed,
> But each in the other blessed.
>
> Him great harmes had taught much care,
> Her faire necke a foule yoke bare,
> But her sight his cares did banish,
> In his sight her yoke did vanish.[3]

Sometimes, however, he is more than this: he is identified with Lord Rich, in some of the most mysterious poems of all. They can, I think, be taken in two contrasting ways. It is easy to see them as poems expressing hate:

> . . . that rich foole, who by blind Fortune's lot
> The richest gemme of Love and life enjoyes,
> And can with foule abuse such beauties blot;
> Let him, deprived of sweet but unfelt joyes,
>   (Exil'd for ay from those high treasures, which
>   He knowes not) grow in only follie rich.[4]

Did Sidney then dislike Lord Rich? Did he ask his friends, when they first saw the poems, to be sure to keep them from Lord Rich? If he did not bother to ask this, why did Rich not, so far as we know, call Sidney out? There is another possibility—that Sidney and Lord Rich were friendly, very friendly, with each other. I do not think that this idea is so absurd as it might at first appear. Strong affection between men, like strong dislike, does sometimes express itself in blatant and often ribald insults. Again, it can be one way of complimenting a man to compliment his wife. How far one can go in this depends on the complexities of the relation between husband and wife and friend, and also on the current etiquette; but if, in the passage I have just quoted, we imagine the words 'foule abuse' to be a hyperbolic reference to some slight annoyance of Rich with his wife, or to some slight neglect of her by him, then the poem as a whole turns into one containing an indirect compliment. This is not, I must stress, to read the poem as primarily biographical, but simply to suggest that the drama of *Astrophil and*

3. *A.S.*, Song 8, lines 5–12, Ringler, p. 218.   4. *A.S.* 24, ibid., p. 177.

Stella may contain such implications. The poem can then be read, and possibly was read by Lord Rich, on two levels: Astrophil's hatred for the obstacle to the enjoyment of his love, and beyond that an amusing reference to some detail in the private life of two of Sidney's friends.[5]

Similarly, the poem on the jealousy of Stella's husband, which does not make the identification with Lord Rich but which might be connected with him in the light of the poems which do, may be read as implying Astrophil's intention to pay Stella's husband out with the greatest injury one man could give another (and that is the primary meaning of the poem in the sequence), and may also be read as containing a friendly warning, not to be taken too seriously, for Lord Rich if the cap fitted:

A monster, other's harme, selfe-miserie,
    Beautie's plague, Vertue's scourge, succour of lies:
    Who his owne joy to his owne hurt applies,
And onely cherish doth with injurie.
    Who since he hath, by Nature's speciall grace,
    So piercing pawes, as spoyle when they embrace,
So nimble feet as stirre still, though on thornes:
    So manie eyes ay seeking their owne woe,
    So ample eares as never good newes know:
Is it not evill that such a Devill wants hornes?[6]

There may, on some of the occasions on which Astrophil speaks about, or with, other acquaintances of his, be allusions to real people and events; but none has been identified. The chief value of the inclusion of these characters is clear: they provide the sense of a world beyond Astrophil's immediate concern with Stella, and so add to the credibility of Astrophil since he is seen so often in a lively social setting. They also make an excellent foil to Astrophil since, when they appear, they are always, in his eyes, in the wrong. One friend uses 'Rubarb words' to warn Astrophil against 'Desire', only to be rebuked for it;[7] another, or perhaps

5. Sidney's and Penelope's families were closely connected (Ringler, pp. 441–2); her brother, the Earl of Essex, one of Sidney's legatees, married Sidney's widow (ibid., p. 443). We do not know whether Sidney was friendly with Lord Rich, for a character sketch of whom see ibid., p. 445. Penelope bore Rich four children, and only became the mistress of Sir Charles Blount two years after Sidney's death (ibid., p. 444).

6. *A.S.* 78, ibid., p. 206.   7. *A.S.* 14, ibid., pp. 171–2.

the same one, is worried lest Astrophil should not fulfil the 'Great expectation' that there is of him, and is dismissed in a similarly cavalier fashion:

Hath this world ought so faire as *Stella* is?[8]

'The curious wits' who try to think of the reason for Astrophil's 'dull pensiveness' are also mocked. Some imagine that he is studying, some that he is concerned with 'state errours', and some 'harder Judges' that he is consumed with ambition; but all are simply wrong:

O fooles, or over-wise, alas the race
Of all my thoughts hath neither stop nor start,
But only *Stella's* eyes and *Stella's* hart.[9]

The next time they, or people very like them, appear they guess wrongly again. This time they think he is proud; but he admits to 'one worse fault, *Ambition*' (a fault he denied previously), only to define it in a way which they would not find acceptable:

That makes me oft my best friends overpasse,
Unseene, unheard, while thought to highest place
Bends all his powers, even unto *Stella's* grace.[1]

Even when his friends guess right, which they manage to do only near the end of the sequence, they are regarded as wrong to do so, because now they are stating the obvious:

. . . if I by a happy window passe,
If I but stars upon mine armour beare,
Sicke, thirsty, glad (though but of empty glasse:)
Your morall notes straight my hid meaning teare
From out my ribs, and puffing prove that I
Do *Stella* love. Fooles, who doth it deny?[2]

As in the previous example, the poem—which seems at first to be expressing Astrophil's misery and his foolishness in the eyes of the world—takes a different direction only in the second part of the last line; then it is the friends who look foolish, with the consequence that Astrophil's passion seems justified.

Astrophil's friends can never do the right thing. When they notice the significance of 'stars upon mine armour' their interpre-

8. *A.S.* 21, ibid., p. 175.   9. *A.S.* 23, ibid., p. 176.
1. *A.S.* 27, ibid., p. 178.   2. *A.S.* 104, ibid., p. 233.

tation is approved, but they are not congratulated on their acumen. This heraldic reference is a pointer to the significance of other heraldic references;[3] yet the friends are sometimes warned against being too 'curious' in their reading:

> You that with allegorie's curious frame,
>> Of other's children changelings use to make,
>> With me those paines for God's sake do not take:
> I list not dig so deepe for brasen fame.
> When I say '*Stella*', I do meane the same
>> Princesse of Beautie, for whose only sake
>> The raines of *Love* I love, though never slake . . .[4]

This, despite the fact that some poems are clearly allegorical,[5] and some contain allusions to Penelope:

> *Cupid* then smiles, for on his crest there lies
>> *Stella's* faire haire, her face he makes his shield,
>> Where roses gueuls are borne in silver field.[6]

The friends are mocked whether they catch the hidden meanings or not, and in all these poems Astrophil is in a sense mocked too, by the strangeness of his behaviour when it is seen against the more generally acceptable standards of the court. Astrophil always has the appropriate images to make his friends' actions seem ridiculous:

> Be your words made (good Sir) of Indian ware,
>> That you allow me them by so small rate?
>> Or do you cutted Spartanes imitate?[7]

But soon Astrophil's excitement, and especially the broken rhythm which expresses it, make him seem ridiculous too:

> When I demaund of *Phenix Stella's* state,
> You say forsooth, you left her well of late.
> O God, thinke you that satisfies my care?
>> I would know whether she did sit or walke,
> How cloth'd, how waited on, sighd she or smilde,
> Whereof, with whom, how often she did talke. . . .[8]

3. See above, pp. 86–7.
4. *A.S.* 28, Ringler, pp. 178–9. See above, pp. 40–1.
5. See above, pp. 33, 38–42.
6. *A.S.* 13, Ringler, p. 171. See above, p. 86.
7. *A.S.* 92, Ringler, p. 225.   8. Ibid.

A similar thing happens in those poems which mention other characters in the drama—the women acquaintances of Astrophil. It seems silly of them to judge of love by the conventional display of it, wearing 'set colours', keeping 'speciall lockes of vowed haire', and giving 'each speech a full point of a grone', and to deny that Astrophil is in love because he does not indulge in this display;[9] but his justification for his lack of demonstrativeness shows him to be as conventional as anyone, for it is a rephrasing of a well-known proverb:[1]

> Dumb Swannes, not chatring Pies, do Lovers prove,
> They love indeed, who quake to say they love.[2]

The tone of this poem is complicated further by Astrophil's mockery of himself as dumb and quaking; in the light of those poems where he is not quaking (clearly, he is not dumb in any of them), this is deliberate false modesty.

Ladies appear later on in the sequence who, by failing to attract Astrophil or at least by failing to distract him, add to the praise of Stella:

> Out traytour absence, darest thou counsell me,
> From my deare Captainesse to run away?
> Because in brave array heere marcheth she,
> That to win me, oft shewes a present pay?[3]

In that poem Astrophil rejects the lady's 'earthly cates'; elsewhere he does find some pleasure in the company of other women than Stella, but even this is—by sheer casuistry and an expedient use of pseudo-platonic notions—turned into a compliment for Stella:

> They please I do confesse, they please mine eyes,
> But why? because of you they models be,
> Models such be wood-globes of glistring skies.
> Deere, therefore be not jealous over me,
>   If you heare that they seeme my hart to move,
>   Not them, ô no, but you in them I love.[4]

Ladies appear in other poems,[5] and attempt to distract Astrophil and fail. They help to fill in the background of the world in which

9. *A.S.* 54, ibid., p. 191.   1. Ibid., p. 476.   2. *A.S.* 54, ibid., p. 192.
3. *A.S.* 88, ibid., p. 223.   4. *A.S.* 91, ibid., p. 225.
5. *A.S.* 97, 106, ibid., pp. 229–30, 235–6.

the drama of *Astrophil and Stella* is set: there is 'store of faire Ladies'[6] in this world, but none like Stella.

Another lady who plays an important part is the first character in the sequence to speak to Astrophil, his Muse:

'Foole,' said my Muse to me, 'looke in thy heart and write.'[7]

She gives her advice brusquely, without waiting to be invoked. Like all the characters in *Astrophil and Stella*, even those representing aspects of Astrophil's mind, she has a certain liveliness and independence. Later in the sequence she is several times invoked:

Sing then my Muse, now *Io Pean* sing.[8]

This may seem strange when we think of Astrophil's frequent insistence that he will have no truck with stylistic ornaments (of which the Muse is surely one of the most obvious); but an interesting distinction is made. Whenever Astrophil speaks of the Muse in an approving way as the personification of his own poetic skill, then she is 'my Muse', in the singular and with that possessive pronoun.[9] Sometimes, however, Astrophil speaks of the Muses, in the plural, with very different effects. He does this when he is praising Stella's 'words, wherein the Muses' treasures be',[1] and when he is praising her lip: 'The new *Pernassus*, where the Muses bide.'[2] The plural form is clearly used to intensify the compliments, and 'The new *Pernassus*' is, I think, meant to contrast with the earlier poem attacking unskilful poets:

You that do search for everie purling spring,
Which from the ribs of old *Parnassus* flowes . . .[3]

The contrast is interesting, because on every other occasion when Astrophil speaks of the Muses in the plural he is either repudiating them as other people's Muses,[4] or casting them off as former companions of his own whom he no longer wishes to associate with,[5]

6. *A.S.* 106, ibid., p. 236.   7. *A.S.* 1, ibid., p. 165.
8. *A.S.* 63, ibid., p. 196; see also *A.S.* 70, lines 9 and 12, Song 5, lines 25 and 32, ibid., pp. 201, 213.
9. *A.S.* 23, line 6, Song 1, lines 1 and 33, *A.S.* 70, line 1, *A.S.*, 77, line 14, *A.S.*, 84, lines 2 and 7, Song 5, line 89, ibid., pp. 176, 196, 197, 201, 205, 209, 215. When the Muse is invoked she is always 'my Muse'; *A.S.* 70, line 12, is only apparently an exception, since the Muse has been addressed as 'my Muse' only three lines previously.
1. *A.S.* 60, ibid., p. 195.   2. *A.S.* 80, ibid., p. 207.
3. *A.S.* 15, ibid., p. 172.   4. *A.S.* 3, 6, 10, ibid., pp. 166, 167, 169.
5. *A.S.* 55, ibid., p. 192.

or else, with a typical mock-modesty which has the same effect, protesting that their company is too good for him to keep:

> I never drank of *Aganippe* well,
> Nor ever did in shade of *Tempe* sit:
> And Muses scorne with vulgar braines to dwell,
> Poore Layman I, for sacred rites unfit.[6]

The single, distinctive Muse of Astrophil, and the other Muses, are actors, then, in the dramatic conflict in the sequence between plainness and ornamentation, between apparent simplicity and artifice.

Like other characters in the sequence, the Muses show different faces according to the poetic needs of the moment. Astrophil's single Muse, for instance, may be confidently invoked as a capable avenger:

> Your Client poore my selfe, shall *Stella* handle so?
> Revenge, revenge, my Muse, Defiance' trumpet blow:
> Threat'n what may be done, yet do more then you threat'n.
> Ah, my sute granted is, I feele my breast doth swell.[7]

Just as easily, her understandable coyness as a single lady may become a way of expressing Astrophil's mock-modesty, so that, after the praise of many of Stella's physical attractions, we have:

> Yet ah, my Mayd'n Muse doth blush to tell the best.[8]

A literary convention, a personification of an abstraction, this Muse may be; but in *Astrophil and Stella* she has, not least because of her varying moods, an individual presence.

A personification which plays an even more important role is Cupid, or 'Love' as he is often called. After Astrophil and Stella themselves, he is the most important person in the drama, no less real because in a sense he represents various aspects of the relationship between them. He makes his entrance in the second poem, first as the soldier who gave Astrophil his wound, and then as the powerful conqueror laying down the law:

> . . . *Love* gave the wound, which while I breathe will bleed . . .
> At length to *Love's* decrees, I forc'd, agreed . . .[9]

6. *A.S.* 74, ibid., p. 203. 7. Song 5, lines 31–4, ibid., p. 213.
8. *A.S.* 77, ibid., p. 205. 9. Ibid., p. 165.

The references in this poem to military affairs ('a dribbed shot', 'mine of time', and 'full conquest') and to ruling ('lost libertie', 'like slave-borne *Muscovite*', and 'to suffer Tyrannie')[1] have the effect of strengthening, of enlivening and individualizing, the personifications in the two lines I have quoted.

After making such an early entrance, Love last appears fully personified near the end, playing a very different role during Stella's sickness:

> Love moves thy paine, and like a faithfull page,
> As thy lookes sturre, runs up and downe to make
> All folkes prest at thy will thy paine to 'swage . . .[2]

And in between he has been seen in many roles, and particularly as a little boy, usually mischievous:

> *Love* still a boy, and oft a wanton is,
> School'd onely by his mother's tender eye:
> What wonder then if he his lesson misse,
> When for so soft a rod deare play he trie?
>   And yet my Starre, because a sugred kisse
> In sport I suckt, while she asleepe did lie,
> Doth lowre, nay, chide; nay, threat for only this:
> Sweet, it was saucie *Love*, not humble I.[3]

There he provides a convenient scapegoat; but his youth does not usually make it easy for Astrophil to cope with him; indeed, his youthful irresponsibility is all the more frightening when we see the power he wields:

> In truth, ô Love, with what a boyish kind
> Thou doest proceed in thy most serious wayes . . .[4]

His power is demonstrated too in other roles: as a horseman, riding Astrophil for the whole length of a sonnet,[5] or in a fleeting appearance riding double:

>   . . . wretch I am constraind,
> (Spurd with love's spur, though gald and shortly raind
> With care's hard hand) to turne and tosse . . .[6]

1. Ibid., pp. 165–6.   2. *A.S.* 101, ibid., p. 232.
3. *A.S.* 73, ibid., p. 203; see also, e.g., *A.S.* 8, 17, 35, 46, ibid., pp. 168, 173, 182, 187.
4. *A.S.* 11, ibid., p. 170.
5. *A.S.* 49, ibid., p. 189, discussed above, pp. 32–3.
6. *A.S.* 98, Ringler, p. 230.

as a teacher:

> O Doctor *Cupid*, thou for me reply . . .[7]

and as a murderer:

> Flie, fly, my friends, I have my death wound; fly,
> See there that boy, that murthring boy I say,
> Who like a theefe, hid in darke bush doth ly,
> Till bloudie bullet get him wrongfull pray.[8]

Sometimes the personification of love is slight and momentary:

> . . . all my words thy beauty doth endite,
> And love doth hold my hand, and makes me write.[9]

At other times the personification is detailed and maintained throughout a poem, as in Sonnet 8 which gives Cupid's life-history,[1] or Sonnet 11 where he is like a child playing with a gorgeous book whose contents he does not understand,[2] or Sonnet 17 where he gets involved in a family squabble.[3] Always, however, he serves the same purpose as the other personifications in the sequence.[4] The style of *Astrophil and Stella* is remarkable for its force and energy, its power not merely to express but also to impress what it says firmly on the reader's mind,[5] and the use of personification is one of the chief reasons for this forcefulness.[6] It is striking how often in his *Apology* Sidney speaks of poetry in dramatic terms:

Poetry . . . is defined largely in terms of dialogue, tales, the motions and whisperings of the people, the 'setting' of a banquet or a walk, and the vivid scenes, actions, or images from dramatic and narrative verse. And these . . . are essentially what Scaliger and Aristotle describe as the main constituents of energia.[7]

It is even more striking how dramatic *Astrophil and Stella* is; the personifications, acting in this drama, have the effect, in Greville's

---

7. *A.S.* 61, ibid., p. 195.   8. *A.S.* 20, ibid., pp. 174–5.
9. *A.S.* 90, ibid., p. 224.   1. Ibid., p. 168.
2. Ibid., p. 170.   3. Ibid., p. 173.
4. e.g., of Nature in *A.S.* 1, 3, 7, 11, 17, 18, ibid., pp. 165, 166, 168, 170, 173; of Virtue in *A.S.* 4, 9, 25, 47, 52, ibid., pp. 166, 169, 177, 188, 190; of Reason in *A.S.* 10, 18, ibid., pp. 169, 173; or Patience in *A.S.* 56, ibid., p. 192. See above, pp. 74–6, for a discussion of Virtue.
5. Rudenstine, pp. 152–62.   6. Montgomery, p. 94.
7. Rudenstine, p. 158.

phrase, of turning 'the barren Philosophy precepts into pregnant Images of life'.[8]

Something we expect in drama is conflict. In *Astrophil and Stella* there is so much conflict, of one sort or another, that almost any discussion of anything in the sequence will be concerned with it. To tease out every little bit of conflict would be tedious, when so many poems are constructed on a framework of 'not this, but that' with a consequent conflict between the two ideas:

> I sought fit words to paint the blackest face of woe . . .
> But words came halting forth . . .[9]

> Not at first sight, nor with a dribbed shot
>   *Love* gave the wound, which while I breathe will bleed:
> But knowne worth did in mine of time proceed . . .[1]

>   Let daintie wits crie on the Sisters nine . . .
>   For me in sooth, no Muse but one I know . . .[2]

> *Vertue* alas, now let me take some rest,
> Thou setst a bate between my will and wit,
> If vaine love have my simple soule opprest,
> Leave what thou likest not, deale not thou with it.[3]

The fifth sonnet is typical of many[4] in the way it is constructed: this is true, so is that, and that, and that, and that, and, in the last line:

> True, and yet true that I must *Stella* love.[5]

In each of these first few sonnets there is more than one kind of conflict. In the first there is not only a conflict between what Astrophil wants to write and his lack of success, but also between the faulty method he adopts and the corrective advice of his Muse.[6] In the second there is not only conflict between the traditional idea of love at first sight and Astrophil's gradual succumbing (a departure from the tradition serious enough to be

8. Greville, op. cit., p. 15. Greville is speaking of incidents in the *Arcadia*.
9. *A.S.* 1, Ringler, p. 165.   1. *A.S.* 2, ibid.
2. *A.S.* 3, ibid., p. 166.   3. *A.S.* 4, ibid.
4. e.g., *A.S.* 6, 12, 21, 30, ibid., pp. 167, 170, 175, 179.
5. Ibid., p. 167.   6. See above, p. 54.

in conflict with it),[7] but also the struggle involved in this gradual succumbing itself. In the third there is not only the conflict between the ornamental style of other poets and Astrophil's own simplicity, but also the clash between what Astrophil says he is doing, writing simply, and what he is also doing in fact— using, to build up his poem, the very ornament he affects to despise.

So one might go on throughout most of the sequence. One might show for a start (and it would be only a start) how the conflicts revealed in the second sonnet are continued in later poems,[8] with Astrophil battling against courtly love-poets,[9] against Stella's coldness towards him,[1] and against 'Vertue'.[2] Rather than go into such detail, which is too much like stating the fairly obvious again and again, I shall concentrate on what seem to me the main conflicts inherent in the whole conception of the sequence.

The dominant conflict is, I think, what has been called the 'dialettica dell'ostacolo':[3] to be an experience worth considering and describing, love has to be obstructed and denied.[4] This is worked out in *Astrophil and Stella* in some detail.[5] In discussing it and emphasizing its importance I do not wish to imply that the main concern of the sequence is with some abstract theme like 'the nature of love', or that the existence of this obstacle to love in the sequence means that love is always obstructed.[6] It is an artistic matter that I am concerned with. To put it at its crudest—when the course of true love runs smooth, then it tends to be so much the less interesting. If even that is too 'philosophical' and generalized, another way of putting it is to say that Sidney has chosen for his subject matter a situation which allows plenty of scope for dramatic conflict.

At first, it seems to me, Astrophil is struggling against a certain

7. Lever, p. 72.

8. Rudenstine, p. 193, sees these conflicts as 'played out primarily in the first twenty-one poems'.

9. e.g., *A.S.* 3, 6, 15, 74, Ringler, pp. 166, 167, 172, 203.

1. e.g., *A.S.* 8, 11, 31, 40, 52, 71, 82, Song 4, Song 8, ibid., pp. 168, 170, 180, 184, 190, 201, 207, 210, 217.

2. See above, pp. 67–70, 72–6.   3. Gentili, p. 160.   4. Ibid.

5. My discussion of this 'dialettica dell'ostacolo' owes much to Gentili, p. 165, although I do not accept as more than approximate the tripartite division of *A.S.* proposed on pp. 151–5.

6. See above, pp. 70–4.

incredulity. Much of his effort is devoted to convincing Stella of his love:

> Thus write I while I doubt to write, and wreake
> My harmes on Ink's poore losse, perhaps some find
> Stella's great powrs, that so confuse my mind.[7]

There is really no 'perhaps' about it: poem after poem ends with a line, often including her name, which relates her to everything that has gone before:

> . . . trembling voice brings forth that I do Stella love.[8]

> . . . Stella behold, and then begin to endite.[9]

> . . . only those two starres in Stella's face.[1]

Astrophil is struggling too with his own incredulity. He is constantly amazed at himself:

> . . . now like slave-borne Muscovite,
> I call it praise to suffer Tyrannie . . .[2]

> I see my course to lose my selfe doth bend:
> I see and yet no greater sorow take,
> Then that I lose no more for Stella's sake.[3]

The very ingenuity of many of these earlier sonnets implies Astrophil's amazement at the situation in which he finds himself, and at the effect which Stella's beauty has on him. He devotes one sonnet, for instance, to wondering why Nature, when she made 'her chief worke, Stella's eyes', coloured them black. He suggests three reasons, agrees with them all, and then says:

> . . . and thus, she minding Love should be
> Placed ever there, gave him this mourning weed,
> To honor all their deaths, who for her bleed.[4]

That such poems often have touches of humour in them[5] only adds to our sense of Astrophil's amazement: he cannot help

7. A.S. 34, Ringler, p. 182.   8. A.S. 6, ibid., p. 168.
9. A.S. 15, ibid., p. 172.   1. A.S. 26, ibid., p. 178.
2. A.S. 2, ibid., p. 166.   3. A.S. 18, ibid., p. 174.
4. A.S. 7, ibid., p. 168.
5. See the discussion of A.S. 9 above, pp. 3–6.

laughing at himself. Astrophil is struggling also with contemporary opinion, sometimes represented by friends of his,[6] and sometimes much more clearly something in his own mind:

> With what sharpe checkes I in my selfe am shent,
>   When into Reason's audite I do go:
>   And by just counts my selfe a banckrout know
> Of all those goods, which heav'n to me hath lent . . .[7]

Later, the main conflict is between Astrophil's desire and Stella's refusal, complicated by the fact that, while refusing him, she lets him understand that she returns his love. I do not wish to suggest a particular point at which this change begins, because *Astrophil and Stella* does not proceed simply in a forward direction,[8] and works often by hints which can be interpreted in different ways. One might argue that Sonnet 44 should be interpreted as expressing Astrophil's desire for the physical consummation of his love:[9]

> My words I know do well set forth my mind,
>   My mind bemones his sense of inward smart;
>   Such smart may pitie claime of any hart,
>   Her heart, sweete heart, is of no Tygre's kind:
>   And yet she heares, yet I no pitty find . . .[1]

On the other hand, we are not told here what evidence of 'pitty' Astrophil wants, while in the sonnet before this the word 'pray' suggests much more strongly to me a desire for the physical consummation of his love:

> Faire eyes, sweet lips, deare heart, that foolish I
> Could hope by *Cupid's* helpe on you to pray;
> Since to himselfe he doth your gifts apply,
> As his maine force, choise sport, and easefull stay.[2]

Certainly by Sonnet 52 Astrophil's desire for the physical consummation of his love cannot be doubted:

> Well *Love*, since this demurre our sute doth stay,
>   Let *Vertue* have that Stella's selfe; yet thus,
>   That *Vertue* but that body graunt to us.[3]

---

6. See above, pp. 97–9.   7. *A.S.* 18, Ringler, p. 173.
8. See below, pp. 112–16.
9. Gentili, p. 153, regards this sonnet as the first poem in the central section, the section in which Astrophil attempts to conquer Stella.
1. Ringler, p. 186.   2. *A.S.* 43, ibid., p. 186.   3. Ibid., p. 191.

After that the conflict continues through many poems. Astrophil's desire is sometimes expressed bluntly:

> . . . while thy beautie drawes the heart to love,
> As fast thy Vertue bends that love to good:
> 'But ah,' Desire still cries, 'give me some food.'[4]

Sometimes it is expressed cheekily:

> Yet those lips so sweetly swelling,
> Do invite a stealing kiss:
> Now will I but venture this,
> Who will read must first learne spelling.[5]

Sometimes it is expressed by elegant innuendo:

> No wind, no shade can coole, what helpe then in my case,
> But with short breath, long lookes, staid feet and walking hed,
> Pray that my sunne go downe with meeker beames to bed.[6]

Stella does relent so far as to allow a kiss,[7] but this only causes more trouble.[8] The fourth song summarizes the conflict very neatly. Stella denies Astrophil:

> Onely joy, now here you are,
> Fit to heare and ease my care:
> Let my whispering voyce obtaine,
> Sweete reward for sharpest paine:
> Take me to thee, and thee to me.
> 'No, no, no, no, my Deare, let be.'[9]

Then, in the last stanza of this song, Stella uses the same words to show her love for him:

> Wo to me, and do you sweare
> Me to hate, but I forbeare?
> Cursed be my destines all,
> That brought me so high to fall:
> Soone with my death I will please thee.
> 'No, no, no, no, my Deare, let be.'[1]

---

4. *A.S.* 71, ibid., p. 201.   5. Song 2, lines 21-4, ibid., p. 203.
6. *A.S.* 76, ibid., p. 205.   7. *A.S.* 81, ibid., p. 207.
8. *A.S.* 82, ibid.   9. Ibid., p. 210.
1. Ibid., p. 211. In the second line of this stanza I have transposed the question mark and comma of the text in Ringler; see Gentili, p. 422, and Muir, review of Ringler, *R.N.* xvi (1963), 232. Other poems which definitely express physical desire are *A.S.* 68, 72, 77, 78, Song 8, Song 9, Ringler, pp. 200, 202, 205, 217, 221.

Towards the end of *Astrophil and Stella* the obstacle in Astrophil's way is Stella's absence. He has been forced to part from her by 'iron lawes of duty';[2] so this conflict is connected with the previous one. Again we must be careful not to divide the sequence too strictly into parts, for Astrophil does see Stella again several times during this period when he writes most often as though he were separated from her:[3] he seems to be present during Stella's sickness,[4] he sees her travelling on the Thames,[5] and he even has a conversation with her from under her window at night.[6] In general, however, these last poems[7] are concerned with Astrophil in a state of 'rigrows exile'.[8] This state he describes as 'a mazefull solitariness',[9] a fine phrase indeed but also one which explains why some of these later poems are disappointing.[1] They lack the dramatic liveliness of so many of the earlier poems, because the earlier characters are usually absent from them. We might say that the obstacle is now so strong that there is little struggle left. There are still personifications, of course:

> ... sorrow comes with such maine rage, that he
> Kils his owne children, teares, finding that they
> By true love were made apt to consort with me.
> Only true sighs, you do not go away,
>   Thanke may you have for such a thankfull part,
>   Thanke-worthiest yet when you shall breake my hart.[2]

But we need only compare that with an earlier example of personification to see how comparatively dull and vague that is. These lines, for instance, with 'bound prentise', 'Trebles sing high', and 'winter liverie' all working together to present love as a person, and all leading up to the last line, yet not so concrete as to

---

2. *A.S.* 87, ibid., p. 222.
3. After *A.S.* 87 poems written as in her absence are *A.S.* 88, 89, 91, 92, Song 10, 97, 98, 104, 106, ibid., pp. 223–7, 229–30, 233, 235.
4. *A.S.* 101 and 102, ibid., pp. 231–2.
5. *A.S.* 103, ibid., p. 232.   6. Song 11, ibid., p. 233.
7. This last section has certainly begun after *A.S.* 87, ibid., p. 222; but one might easily argue that the two previous poems, Song 8 and Song 9, ibid., pp. 217, 221, are part of it.
8. *A.S.* 104, ibid., p. 233.   9. *A.S.* 96, ibid., p. 229.
1. See above, p. 67.   2. *A.S.* 95, Ringler, p. 229.

obscure the concept involved, are not at all exceptional in *Astrophil and Stella*:

> Sonets be not bound prentise to annoy:
> Trebles sing high, as well as bases deepe:
> Griefe but *Love's* winter liverie is, the Boy
> Hath cheekes to smile, as well as eyes to weepe.[3]

There are poems among the last ones as good as any in the sequence,[4] but generally much of the life has gone out of it with a stronger sense of despair having come in.

It is interesting, and I think it points to something important in *Astrophil and Stella*, that a critic who regards some of these later poems as weak can still find a justification for their inclusion: '. . . the characteristic weaknesses of the poems have a dramatic effect in the context as the symbolic vehicle for the helpless frustration of the lover.'[5] This is not the first time we have met such an argument,[6] and I think there is something in it. It is based on the belief, completely justified in my opinion, that the sequence is not just a random collection but must be seen as a whole to which even the weaker poems contribute something of value. It is similar to saying, as we can say with Sidney, that even the weaker single lines in individual poems are partly justified in that they forward the meaning of the poems in which they occur. The justification is, however, only partial: we still wish that single lines and whole poems could be effective also in themselves, as so many lines and whole poems in *Astrophil and Stella* are. Pushed very far, the argument is a dangerous one. There is a difference between a lover's frustration and a poet's: a poet, as poet, is frustrated when he cannot write effectively and is therefore so much less a poet. Even, for instance, a poem on the subject of dullness should not be dull. True, one line in a play may be in itself flat but in its context striking, like Lear's famous

> Pray you, undo this button: thank you, Sir.[7]

---

3. *A.S.* 70, ibid., p. 201.   4. e.g., *A.S.* 92 and 103, ibid., pp. 225, 232.
5. Young, p. 85. The comment is on *A.S.* 94–103, with the exception of *A.S.* 99: I do not regard *A.S.* 99 as an exception, and I do not regard *A.S.* 103 as a weak poem.
6. See above, pp. 66–7.
7. *King Lear*, v.iii.309, ed. Kenneth Muir, 1955, p. 218.

Nevertheless, there is difference between this and a whole speech of, say, thirty flat lines, so many that their flatness predominates over any dramatic appropriateness they may have. There is also, despite my emphasis on the dramatic qualities of *Astrophil and Stella*, some difference between a stage-play and a set of sonnets.

It is clearly time to consider how far *Astrophil and Stella* should be looked upon as a continuous narrative. I have already quoted with approval[8] Nashe's summary of the action: 'The argument cruell chastitie, the Prologue hope, the Epilogue dispaire. . . .'[9] This suggests some narrative progression in the sequence, but it does not commit itself on detail. This is just as well, since the matter is complicated immediately we realize, for instance, that Sonnets 69–72 form a miniature version of the sequence as a whole.[1]

It is not uncommon to read *Astrophil and Stella* as a sequence with 'a continuous narrative thread';[2] but once we go into detail we find, not just 'one or two inconsistencies',[3] but serious difficulties in reading it in this way. Even critics who agree on dividing the sequence into three parts, and more or less agree on what each part is about, do not make their divisions in the same places.[4] Then, while we are wondering whether the second part begins with Sonnet 44[5] or Sonnet 52,[6] we may remember that some see a second movement beginning with Sonnet 33.[7] The implication here is that Sonnet 33 is a better poem than any of its predecessors. I doubt whether this is true, but the implication does bring into play an important consideration. If there is a conflict between the two, should we concentrate on those sonnets which seem to us to be the best poems, or should we concentrate on those which forward the narrative?

I think there can be only one answer to this. For all our awareness that there is narrative in *Astrophil and Stella*, and for all our attempts to follow it closely, we find ourselves remembering, and

8. Above, p. 80.   9. Nashe, op. cit., p. 223.
1. Kalstone, p. 174.   2. Montgomery, p. 78.
3. Ibid.   4. Gentili, pp. 150–5; Ringler, pp. xlvi-xlix.
5. Gentili, p. 153.   6. Ringler, p. xlvii.
7. See above, p. 59. Hamilton, 'Sidney's *Astrophel and Stella* as a Sonnet Sequence', *E.L.H.* xxxvi (1969), 59–87, suggests that a second stage begins at *A.S.* 36, and a third at *A.S.* 72 (ibid., 67). I do not find the arguments for this exact division convincing; but the essay is valuable as showing many of the ways in which different sonnets are related to each other (69–87).

thinking most about, those poems which insist on drawing attention to themselves simply by being the best poems. In detail, the narrative is not continuous, except in some groups of poems,[8] and many poems make very satisfactory little narratives in themselves and would do even if they were read by themselves.[9] There is a danger that, if we concentrate on the narrative as a whole, which after all depends on a comparatively small number of poems,[1] we may overvalue some poems simply because they forward the narrative. The best reason for reading the sequence is to enjoy its imaginative achievement, and surely this should predominate in our response.[2] As an instance, Sonnet 87[3] is important because it makes it plain that Astrophil and Stella are separated; but is it as interesting, as good a poem, as Sonnet 92[4] which, although it is one of a group written as though during Stella's absence,[5] could easily have been placed elsewhere in the sequence? I am not arguing that the order of the poems is unimportant, but that it is not always so exactly right that it might not have been different. *Astrophil and Stella* is remarkably well organized for a sonnet-sequence; but the fact that it is a sonnet-sequence should remind us that it is not primarily a narrative poem.

It is generally agreed that *Astrophil and Stella* ends inconclusively:[6] Astrophil still wants to consummate his love, he is still unable to, and he is left lamenting:

> So strangely (alas) thy works in me prevaile,
> That in my woes for thee thou art my joy,
> And in my joyes for thee my only annoy.[7]

The sequence breaks off short, or rather, since the last few poems are very far from being among the best, it tails away. Would anyone consider this a satisfactory ending to a narrative poem or to a play? The sequence begins by plunging *in medias res* with Astrophil already in love,[8] and some later poems are in the nature of

8. Cooper, op. cit., p. 31.
9. e.g., *A.S.* 8, 13, 17, 20, 41, 53, Ringler, pp. 168, 171, 173, 174, 185, 191.
1. Castley, op. cit., pp. 60–1.   2. Ibid., p. 62.   3. Ringler, p. 222.
4. Ibid., p. 225.   5. See above, p. 110, footnote 3.
6. Kalstone, p. 178; Lever, p. 82; Montgomery, p. 117.
7 *A.S.* 108, Ringler, p. 237.
8. *A.S.* 1, ibid., p. 165: 'Loving in truth, and faine in verse my love to show . . .'

flashbacks to show how he arrived where he is.[9] This by itself would not prohibit a clear narrative progression, since it is a frequent device in narratives; but it does at least warn us from the start that there is no simple forward movement in the sequence.

The two basic facts are, I think, these: *Astrophil and Stella* manages, among other things, to tell a more coherent story than any other Elizabethan sonnet-sequence; and *Astrophil and Stella* is a set of sonnets (with some songs interspersed), and the sonnet is, perhaps more than any other verse-form, inclined to be self-contained:[1] we should not read each sonnet as though it were a stanza in a narrative poem. The clash between these two facts is largely responsible for one of the most striking features of *Astrophil and Stella*: many of the poems in it are very successful when read by themselves and seem to need nothing else with them, and yet we find that they are even better when read in their context.[2]

When I suggest that the sonnet is basically a self-contained poem, I am not referring especially to the rhyme-scheme, although Sidney's frequent use of the couplet-ending[3]—or better perhaps, despite the frequency of couplet-endings—his frequent use of the final line to round a poem off[4] does support my argument. It would be unwise to attach too much significance to rhyme-schemes. A form with a much more elaborate rhyme-scheme than the sonnet—the Spenserian stanza—is, in the hands of its originator at least, an excellent vehicle for narrative. Spenser is often working against the natural tendency of his stanza to round itself off at the end and complete the fulfilment of our expectations; he uses numerous devices to link his stanzas.[5] It all depends on what a poet does with the form he chooses. The sonnet has a distinctive feel which, after more than four hundred years of use in English and despite its wide variety of rhyme-schemes, means that it still makes sense to talk of the sonnet as one thing. Its rhyme-schemes are various, its subject matter is various, and it has been used by poets of very different gifts; but its dominant characteristic

9. e.g., *A.S.* 2 and 16, ibid., pp. 165, 172.   1. Castley, op. cit., pp. 60–1.
2. e.g., *A.S.* 39, Ringler, p. 184. See Muir, *Sir Philip Sidney*, pp. 33–4.
3. Craik, op. cit., pp. 9–10.
4. Kalstone, p. 123. See also above, p. 36.
5. For some examples see Edmund Spenser, *The Mutabilitie Cantos*, ed. S. P. Zitner, 1968, p. 63.

through all this is to seem complete and rounded off at the end. The close of Sonnet 71 is typical:

> So while thy beautie drawes the heart to love,
> As fast thy Vertue bends that love to good:
> 'But ah,' Desire still cries, 'give me some food.'[6]

There is a dramatic clash in this sonnet between two kinds of love, love as a purifying and ennobling emotion, and love as physical desire,[7] and this is a conflict played out in many other poems in the sequence, so that this poem gains when read in its context. At the same time, the poem in itself does not ask us to read on. The last line does not hold us in suspense waiting for the next poem; rather it turns back on all that has gone before in this poem and transforms our reaction to it: what seemed at first to be a celebration of chastity turns into a neat, and completed, dramatization of a psychological conflict.[8] As a person Astrophil is in a frustrated condition, with his problem stated but not resolved. The poem, on the other hand, which is entirely concerned with stating the problem by holding two opposing ideas in tension, is complete and unfrustrated and entirely satisfying in itself.

This poem, like others in the sequence, does not *need* anything beyond itself; but it gets, as a bonus, one hundred and eighteen other poems to keep it company, and it does gain from their presence. Almost as striking as the power of individual poems is the imaginative fertility over the whole range,[9] the ability, for instance, to play other variations on the theme of unsatisfied desire.[1] The sonnet-sequence is not basically a way of telling a story, but rather a means of meditating on one main experience and seeing it in different lights, with, also, frequent digressions from the main theme.[2] We have, then, 'shifts of viewpoint rather than . . . narrative progression'.[3] The word 'rather' is important, because there is narrative; but narrative is not the most important thing. Sidney manages to make his sequence add up to more than the sum of its parts, he gives a set of lyrics some of the cohesion and order of larger forms,[4] by careful and imaginative planning,[5] at least by planning more careful and imaginative than we usually

6. Ringler, p. 201. 7. Kalstone, p. 119. 8. Castley, op. cit., pp. 62–3.
9. Kalstone, p. 105. 1. See above, pp. 108–9.
2. Castley, op. cit., p. 63; Lewis, *English Literature in the Sixteenth Century*, p. 327.
3. Kalstone, p. 133. 4. Montgomery, p. 119. 5. Howell, op. cit., p. 187.

have in a sonnet-sequence, by frequent cross-references between the poems, and by making even the apparent digressions relevant to the main theme. Instances are everywhere. Sonnet 30, concerned for eleven of its lines with political matters, is perhaps chiefly interesting for what it says about those matters; but is it ultimately a political poem? In the last three lines the apparent digression is stated to be a digression, and so, paradoxically, ceases to be one:

> These questions busie wits to me do frame;
> I, cumbred with good maners, answer do,
> But know not how, for still I thinke of you.[6]

Also, when the poem is read in its context, is it not true that, as we read the first eleven lines, we are waiting to see how even this will be brought round to Stella? We have seen this sort of movement before,[7] and, still better prepared for it by Sonnet 30, we shall see it again.[8]

Indeed, much of the unity of the sequence is due to the recurrence of themes and imagery. Those personifications which appear several times[9] naturally have the effect of making us relate one poem to another, since we are interested in seeing how the same personification will behave in different circumstances. Again, the many references to horsemanship, for instance,[1] help to give the poems a common atmosphere. It is not simply that literal horses often appear in the poems as part of Astrophil's chivalric world:

> Having this day my horse, my hand, my launce
> Guided so well, that I obtain'd the prize . . .[2]

> In Martiall sports I had my cunning tride,
> And yet to breake more staves did me addresse . . .
> One hand forgott to rule, th'other to fight.[3]

Horses are so much a part of this world, and of Astrophil's interests, that he often goes to them for his imagery:

> The raines of *Love* I love, though never slake . . .[4]

6. Ringler, p. 180. 7. e.g., *A.S.* 15, 23, ibid., pp. 172, 176.
8. e.g., *A.S.* 37, 39, 41, 55, ibid., pp. 183, 184, 185, 192.
9. See above, pp. 101–5. 1. See above, pp. 32–3.
2. *A.S.* 41, Ringler, p. 185.
3. *A.S.* 53, ibid., p. 191. See also *A.S.* 22 and 84, ibid., pp. 175, 209.
4. *A.S.* 28, ibid., p. 179. See also *A.S.* 21, lines 5–6, ibid., p. 175; *A.S.* 58, lines 3–4, ibid., p. 194; *A.S.* 102, lines 9–10, ibid., p. 232.

There are many other recurrent themes and images, of course. To attempt to draw up complete and carefully defined lists of them would, however, be misleading. The line I quoted last not only uses imagery drawn from horsemanship, but also contains an example of the frequent personification of love and (in the same word) an example of Cupid being used as part of the mythological machinery of the sequence, or, if we like, as one of the characters in the drama. The different themes and images are interwoven, and it is often not even possible to make a firm distinction between what is a theme and what is an image. In addition, once we have said all that, we still miss the main point of that line if we fail to see that, since Astrophil is by implication compared to a horse, the dominant effect is one of witty self-mockery. Dangers are always there when we isolate (as we often must) one aspect of poetry for discussion; but imagery is particularly resistant to being placed in categories. I shall merely suggest some of the main themes and kinds of imagery used, in order to emphasize, what I hope is already apparent from much of what I have said, how closely knit the sequence is imaginatively.

The recurrent use of Petrarchan themes and images is important as a means of binding the different poems together, and it is important also because it helps to establish a background of conventional love against which Astrophil's individuality stands out. Very many Petrarchan themes and images are employed:[5] Stella's eyes are compared to stars;[6] her hair is golden,[7] and her skin is white;[8] her voice is heavenly music;[9] her actions are those of a goddess;[1] her lover burns in hell;[2] he suffers from wounds which are described as those of battle, especially siege-warfare;[3] his heart is a theatre of civil war;[4] he is often on the verge of death;[5] and night, which for him is a symbol of death, is also an occasion for images of his lady to appear.[6]

The images are entwined with each other, often in a very interesting manner. For instance, the image of Stella's eyes as

---

5. In listing these themes and images, but not in exemplifying them, I have drawn on Montgomery, pp. 53–4.
6. e.g., *A.S.* 26, line 14, Ringler, p. 178.
7. e.g., *A.S.* 9, line 4, ibid., p. 169. 8. e.g., *A.S.* 9, line 3, ibid.
9. e.g., Song 7, lines 17–18, ibid., p. 217.
1. e.g., Song 1, lines 13–16, ibid., p. 197.
2. e.g., *A.S.* 100, line 8, ibid., p. 231. 3. e.g., *A.S.* 2, lines 1–4, ibid., p. 165.
4. e.g., *A.S.* 39, lines 5–7, ibid., p. 184.
5. e.g., *A.S.* 20, line 1, ibid., p. 174. 6. e.g., *A.S.* 32, ibid., pp. 180–1.

stars, as givers of light, is used in different ways, not only to give the sequence unity,[7] but also to give it variety. When she looks on while Astrophil jousts, then she improves his performance;[8] but when he looks at her during a tournament he is dazzled and performs discreditably.[9] On both occasions the image of Stella's eyes as givers of light is combined with equine imagery and with imagery of fighting. As always in poetry, however, what matters most is how the imagery is used; and that point can be emphasized here if we consider why one of these poems is so much better than the other. 'Having this day my horse, my hand, my launce'[1] suffers from one of the worst defects a sonnet can have. After being for most of its length an extremely lively poem—with five sets of people suggesting different reasons for Astrophil's success in the tournament, reasons which are neatly appropriate to those who suggest them—it sinks lamentably in the last three lines:

> How farre they shoote awrie! the true cause is,
>   *Stella* lookt on, and from her heavenly face
>   Sent forth the beames, which made so faire my race.[2]

To a modern these lines may well seem vague. How could Stella's eyes affect Astrophil's performance? The trouble is really that the lines are in a way too precise and limited. Sidney is here making use of a quasi-scientific notion of his time, the notion of ocular fascination, the spirit, 'a lucid, subtle vapour generated out of the purer blood by the heat of the heart',[3] being emitted from the eyes to work a physical change on those whom it strikes. There is no mention in the poem of any psychological reaction by Astrophil; the effect could have come about (and, in the light of the other sonnet where his looking at Stella has disastrous effects, must have come about) without his being aware of its cause at the time. The effectiveness of Sidney's lines is, then, one of the casualties of time and change. If we are no longer able to accept the notion of ocular fascination as a physical process, we are also unable, in this instance, to take the lines figuratively in any satisfying way. In

7. John, op. cit., pp. 152–4.   8. *A.S.* 41, Ringler, p. 185.
9. *A.S.* 53, ibid., p. 191.   1. *A.S.* 41, ibid., p. 185.
2. Ibid.   3. Craig, op. cit., pp. 43–4.

the other sonnet, 'In Martiall sports I had my cunning tride',[4] which may well have been based on the same idea originally, no such problem arises, since what happens is easily appreciable in terms of a psychological influence; Astrophil was overcome with emotion, and consequently confused:

> I look'd, and *Stella* spide,
> Who hard by made a window send forth light.
> My heart then quak'd, then dazled were mine eyes,
> One hand forgott to rule, th'other to fight.[5]

We need, perhaps, to accept some comic hyperbole; but this is not difficult when Astrophil is throughout the poem mocking himself

> In *Marse's* liverie, prauncing in the presse . . .[6]

As with the narrative elements in *Astrophil and Stella*, the most important thing is not what can be found in the sequence, but what is most effective poetically.[7]

For this reason we can easily accept the movement from Stella's eyes as givers of an influential light to the idea that she shoots from them 'sweete cruell shot'.[8] This image, also a comically hyperbolic one in its context, connects easily with that of Cupid's arrows:

> . . . her eyes
> Serve him with shot . . .[9]

As that suggests, it is often doubtful who is responsible for the shooting:

> Not at first sight, nor with a dribbed shot
> *Love* gave the wound, which while I breathe will bleed . . .[1]

'*Love*', or Cupid, is here an aspect of Stella. Frequent references to Cupid's arrows[2] connect naturally with images of warfare,[3] and those with images of conquest[4] and slavery.[5]

4. *A.S.* 53, Ringler, p. 191.   5. Ibid.   6. Ibid.
7. See above, pp. 112–13.   8. *A.S.* 48, Ringler, p. 189.
9. *A.S.* 29, ibid., p. 179.   1. *A.S.* 2, ibid., p. 165.
2. e.g., *A.S.* 5, 8, 14, 17, 20, 31, ibid., pp. 167, 168, 171, 173, 174, 180.
3. e.g., *A.S.* 2, 12, 22, 29, 36, 39, 40, 48, 55, 88, 98, ibid., pp. 165, 171, 176, 179, 182, 184, 185, 189, 192, 223, 230.
4. e.g., *A.S.* 2, 29, 40, ibid., pp. 165, 179, 185.
5. e.g., *A.S.* 2, 47, ibid., pp. 166, 188.

Recurrent themes and images, then, help to unify the sequence, but not in any mechanical way.

> Weigh then how I by thee am overthrowne:
>> And then, thinke thus, although thy beautie be
>> Made manifest by such a victorie,
> Yet noblest Conquerours do wreckes avoid.
>> Since then thou hast so farre subdued me,
>> That in my heart I offer still to thee,
> O do not let thy Temple be destroyd.[6]

Those lines connect with many other poems, since they contain the ideas of warfare, and of Stella conquering, a hint of slavery, and also the implication that Stella is a goddess. Most important, however, is how these themes and implications are combined in an effect which is both a serious statement of Astrophil's psychological state and, by the hyperbole involved, a comic commentary on this state.[7]

The inclusion in *Astrophil and Stella* of eleven songs, whose most obvious effect is to give the sequence more variety, does not impair its unity. It has been objected that, although they certainly should be distributed in the sequence, they would be better if they were distributed differently.[8] Objections have even been made which imply that it would be better if some of them were omitted.[9] Now, I think it is true that, if all these songs had been lost, or never written, no one would have suspected that something was missing. *Astrophil and Stella* is well planned, I think, but not so well planned that nothing could have been omitted from it without its absence being apparent; and many of the poems in it, sonnets as well as songs, could easily be in different places. I think it is of the nature of a sequence like this, a number of meditations on the one main experience, that there can hardly be an inevitable order for the separate poems which compose it. This does not mean, however, that they are not effectively placed where they stand. It is significant that those who are uneasy about some of the songs are not necessarily uneasy about the same ones. A. R. Howe suggests that four songs[1] are in their right places, while the others need

6. *A.S.* 40, ibid., p. 185.
7. For a discussion relevant to this combination, without inconsistency, of diverse images, see above, pp. 30–3.
8. Howe, op. cit., pp. 164–7.   9. Ringler, pp. xlv–vi.
1. Songs 2, 5, 10, 11, ibid., pp. 202, 212, 225, 233.

redistributing.[2] William J. Ringler is happy about only three of these,[3] but suggests another three which seem to him effective in themselves and also rightly placed.[4]

The latter's arguments are interesting. The six songs which satisfy him are those which he thinks narrate important events;[5] those which do not narrate important events he regards as 'little more than fillers'.[6] The grouping, between two songs concerned with meetings of Astrophil and Stella, of Sonnet 86[7] and three other songs,[8] none of them narrative, he regards as clumsy, and justified only by the need to separate the two important meetings. He admits that the 'change of lookes' of Sonnet 86 occasions the reproaches of Song 5, but says that this 'change of lookes' comes strangely after Stella's revelation of her affection for Astrophil in Song 4 which immediately precedes Sonnet 86. Songs 6 and 7 are admitted to be related to each other, since both of them are about Stella's voice and face, but are said to come strangely after the reproaches of Song 5, and to make no preparation for the meeting in Song 8. These objections lose much of their force if we are not attempting to find in *Astrophil and Stella* a well-defined and consistent narrative structure which is not meant to be there.[9]

It is much better to see the songs, rather like the sonnets, as poems which are all intended to be satisfying in themselves, while each has also a certain dramatic value in the sequence as a whole. In some ways they are rather like the songs in a play by Shakespeare, which mark pauses in the action and sum up the mood of the moment:[1] 'Like the *Arcadia* lyrics they are set pieces, abstracting emotions from the main flow of the sequence and giving them a more emphatic and extended voice.'[2] That is the main function of all the songs (even those which are more or less narrative in form); but the ways in which they perform this function vary, and each song is worth discussing in a little more detail.

2. Howe, op. cit., p. 167.
3. He disagrees about Song 5; see Ringler, pp. xlv–vi.
4. These three are Songs 4, 8, 9, ibid., pp. 210, 217, 221.
5. Ibid., p. xlv.
6. Ibid. My summary of his arguments is drawn from ibid., pp. xlv–vi.
7. Ibid., p. 212.
8. Songs 5, 6, 7, ibid., pp. 212, 215, 217.
9. See above, pp. 112–16.
1. Buxton, *Sir Philip Sidney and the English Renaissance*, p. 185.
2. Montgomery, p. 86.

Song 1, 'Doubt you to whom my Muse these notes entendeth',[3]
follows quite naturally after the joy expressed in the poem before:

> Sing then my Muse, now *Io Pean* sing,
> Heav'ns envy not at my high triumphing . . .[4]

Appropriately, as a set piece dwelling on this emotion, it has an
elaborately ritualistic movement:[5]

> Who hath the haire which, loosest, fastest tieth,
> Who makes a man live then glad when he dieth?
> To you, to you, all song of praise is due:
> Only of you the flatterer never lieth.[6]

This ritualistic formality, undramatic in itself, becomes dramatic
in contrast with the preceding sonnet.[7] It is, of course, true of all
the songs that, by their verse-form alone, they contrast dramatically with the sonnets.

Song 2, 'Have I caught my heav'nly jewell',[8] also follows neatly
from its preceding sonnet. That sonnet is concerned, as so many
are, with a conflict:

> Service and Honor, wonder with delight,
> Feare to offend, will worthie to appeare,
> Care shining in mine eyes, faith in my sprite,
> These things are left me by my only Deare;
> But thou Desire, because thou wouldst have all,
> Now banisht art, but yet alas how shall?[9]

The conflict discussed in that sonnet, dramatically indeed but still
only discussed, is, in the song, shown in action in a particular
situation:

> Her tongue waking still refuseth,
> Giving frankly niggard No:
> Now will I attempt to know,
> What No her tongue sleeping useth.
>
> See the hand which waking gardeth,
> Sleeping, grants a free resort:
> Now will I invade the fort;
> Cowards *Love* with losse rewardeth.

3. Ringler, p. 196.   4. *A.S.* 63, ibid.   5. Gentili, p. 364; above, pp. 28–9.
6. Ringler, p. 197.   7. Young, p. 81.   8. Ringler, p. 202.
9. *A.S.* 72, ibid.

Also, the song, with its following two sonnets,[1] gives us the episode or episodes in which Astrophil kisses Stella, so providing a theme which, after an interval, will be developed in Sonnets 79–82.[2] This is a good instance of how the 'narrative' works: a theme is introduced, developed a little, and apparently left (only apparently left, because there is some relation to the kiss theme even in the intervening sonnets, since they are all very sensual),[3] and then taken up once more and developed at some length.

It is probable that Sonnet 83,[4] the warning to 'brother *Philip*', is, in its relevance to Astrophil and probably to Sidney too,[5] meant to be part of the group on the theme of the kiss.[6] It is certainly related to the song which follows it, 'If Orpheus' voyce had force to breathe such musicke's love',[7] in a dramatic way by sheer contrast. There is a contrast in theme—against the warning to the sparrow is the lyrical celebration of Stella's charms; there is also a contrast in manner—the stylization of the song against the colloquialism of the sonnet. Such dramatic juxtapositions as this, rather than a consistently developing narrative, are what enable us to describe *Astrophil and Stella* as a dramatic work. The clash between these two poems—in a sense their inappropriateness to each other—is exactly what makes them appropriate in a sequence concerned so much with the conflicts in Astrophil's mind.

Song 4, 'Onely joy, now here you are',[8] is of special importance even if we do not agree wholeheartedly that it marks a definite stage in the narrative as the end of the second part and the beginning of the third.[9] It summarizes one of the main conflicts in the sequence, that between Astrophil's desire and Stella's chastity while she admits her love:[1] it looks back, therefore, to the poems of desire,[2] and also forward to Astrophil's separation from Stella by 'iron lawes of duty'.[3]

Song 5, 'While favour fed my hope, delight with hope was brought',[4] an 'attack' on Stella for her ill usage of Astrophil, does not, in my opinion, come very strangely after the revelation of Stella's affection in Song 4. In Song 4 Stella does not merely

1. *A.S.* 73, 74, ibid., p. 203.
2. Ibid., pp. 206–8. The point is made in Gentili, p. 384.
3. Gentili, p. 384.   4. Ringler, p. 208.   5. See above, p. 87.
6. *A.S.* 79–82, Ringler, pp. 206–8.   7. Song 3, ibid., p. 208.
8. Ibid., p. 210.   9. As argued in Gentili, pp. 154–5.
1. See above, p. 109.   2. See above, pp. 108–9.
3. *A.S.* 87, Ringler, p. 222. See above, pp. 110–11.   4. Ringler, p. 212.

reveal affection, but also insists that she will not return Astrophil's love physically, and his last words in that song show him far from pleased:

> Cursed be my destines all,
> That brought me so high to fall:
> Soone with my death I will please thee.[5]

Also, another sonnet, complaining of Stella's 'change of lookes',[6] intervenes between Song 4 and Song 5. Most important of all, we are satisfied if we wish for psychological aptness rather than an obvious narrative progression. The 'attack' on Stella may be intended as a joke: whether it is a joke or not, it is understandable and artistically acceptable as a very natural reaction by Astrophil to his sexual frustration.

Song 6, 'O you that heare this voice',[7] and Song 7, 'Whose senses in so evill consort, their stepdame Nature laies',[8] are both, since they praise Stella highly, very appropriate followers to Song 5. All three poems bear witness, although in different ways, to the great effect Stella has on Astrophil, and that is surely the point here.

Song 8, 'In a grove most rich of shade',[9] is distinctive as the only poem in the sequence written in the third person. One way of accounting for this is to suggest that it was originally written separately without the thought of its being included in *Astrophil and Stella*.[1] Whatever the origins of this song, however, its peculiarity makes for a valuable artistic effect. The use of the third person and the past tense makes the poem a flashback to some event in the past,[2] seen now by Astrophil with greater objectivity as from a distance.[3] The song is a striking warning against our trying to see in every poem some straightforward development of the story.[4] The shift of viewpoint here, intensified by the biographical intrusion at the end of the song,[5] is perhaps a more drastic one than any elsewhere; but it is only one of many shifts of viewpoint in the sequence.

Song 9, 'Go my flocke, go get you hence',[6] which follows immediately after Song 8, continues to give this distancing effect, but

---

5. Ringler, p. 211.   6. *A.S.* 86, ibid., p. 212.   7. Ibid., p. 215.
8. Ibid., p. 217.   9. Ibid.
1. Ibid., p. xlvi. In the same place this explanation is also suggested for the use of the pastoral convention in Song 9.
2. Gentili, p. 439.   3. Young, p. 77.   4. Gentili, p. 439.
5. See above, pp. 93–4.   6. Ringler, p. 221.

uses a different method. This method is the pastoral guise lent to
Astrophil and Stella. I do not think this is an inconsistency in the
sequence.[7] It is partially prepared for by the Maytime setting of the
preceding song, and by the manner in which that song too sets
Astrophil and Stella at a sort of distance from the reader. More
important, the pastoral convention was then so well established
that any poet could easily slip into it (not as one slips into a skid,
but as one slips into clothes), and it must be understood as a
deliberately remote way of speaking of a poet-lover and his lady.[8]
It would be absurd to take it literally, and indeed in this poem that
can only be done by imagining a real shepherd who, despite the
fact that he must be well acquainted with sheep, thinks them
capable of understanding what he says:

> Leave a wretch, in whom all wo
> Can abide to keepe no measure,
> Merry flocke, such one forgo,
> Unto whom mirth is displeasure,
> Only rich in mischiefe's treasure.
>
> Yet alas before you go,
> Heare your wofull maister's story . . .[9]

Song 10, 'O deare life, when shall it be',[1] concerned with
imagining the pleasure of meeting Stella again, both follows
naturally from the sonnet which precedes it,[2] in which Astrophil
is begging a friend who has seen Stella to talk more about her, and,
with its simpler, more rapid movement and its almost ecstatic
feeling, contrasts with the wry colloquialism of that sonnet:

> Thought see thou no place forbeare,
> Enter bravely every where,
> Seaze on all to her belonging;
> But if thou wouldst garded be,
> Fearing her beames, take with thee
> Strength of liking, rage of longing.

7. As suggested ibid., p. xlvi.   8. See above, pp. 39–40.
9. Song 9, lines 6–12, Ringler, p. 221.   1. Ibid., p. 225.
2. A.S. 92, ibid.

Thinke of that most gratefull time,
    When my leaping hart will clime,
    In my lips to have his biding,
    There those roses for to kisse,
    Which do breath a sugred blisse,
    Opening rubies, pearles deviding.[3]

Song 11, 'Who is it that this darke night',[4] breaks dramatically into the group of poems written as in Stella's absence with its recording of a conversation between Astrophil and Stella. In one sense, then, the song comes as a shock; but it is appropriately placed, since Stella's harshness to Astrophil here, in contrast to her earlier unwilling refusal of him in Song 4,[5] provides some of the background for the lamenting sonnets which surround it. The change which has taken place in their relationship is shown subtly by the differences between this song and Song 4. Both songs are entirely in dialogue, but in Song 4 Astrophil is the petitioner and given most of the words, while Stella refuses him with the same line at the end of each stanza:

'No, no, no, no, my Deare, let be.'[6]

Also, as I have already pointed out,[7] that line of refusal changes its meaning, at the very end of the poem, into an admission of affection for Astrophil. In Song 11, the positions are in a way reversed. Here Stella, who speaks much more than she does in the other poem, is the petitioner, petitioning Astrophil to go away. At the end, too, he is dismissed, not by an ambiguous line which contains as much affection as dismissal, but quite brusquely:[8]

'Peace, I thinke that some give eare:
Come no more, least I get anger.'
Blisse, I will my blisse forbeare,
Fearing (sweete) you to endanger,
But my soule shall harbour there.

---

3. Song 10, lines 19–30, ibid., p. 226.   4. Ibid., p. 233.
5. Ibid., pp. 210–11.   6. Ibid.   7. See above, p. 109.
8. Young, pp. 85–6, quoted with approval in Gentili, p. 494.

'Well, be gone, be gone I say,
Lest that *Argus* eyes perceive you.'
O unjustest fortune's sway,
Which can make me thus to leave you,
And from lowts to run away. [9]

With the songs, as with the sonnets, I have deliberately avoided
discussing whether the incidents which they present ever actually
happened. No one knows; and as readers of poetry we are most
properly concerned with what was made of each experience, real
or imagined. Song 9,[1] in which Astrophil is presented as a shepherd and Stella as a shepherdess, is only a particularly striking
instance of a procedure we find throughout *Astrophil and Stella*
where

True hearts, clear heads will hear the note of glory
And put inverted commas round the story. . . .[2]

Song 9, indeed, needs to be read with several sets of inverted
commas imagined round it. The act of writing a poem implies one
set if we remember that the poet is 'making things either better
than Nature bringeth forth, or, quite anew, forms such as never
were in Nature',[3] the attribution of the poem and the feelings in it
to a fictional character—Astrophil—implies another set, and the
temporary metamorphosis of Astrophil, usually shown as a
courtier, into a shepherd implies a third set. The question which
is bound to arise—how far the reader is willing to follow the
author in this highly artificial procedure—involves a discussion
which cannot be avoided. We need to consider what sort of
reader Sidney seems to have had in mind, and also how the poems
should be read by someone, like ourselves, whom Sidney cannot
have had specifically in mind.

Several kinds of reader are involved. First there is possibly the
person addressed in a poem, when it does address someone,
although we must not too lightly assume that a poet intends his
poem to be read first, if at all, by someone to whom he addresses
it: this person may be Stella,[4] or an unnamed friend[5] or friends.[6]

9. Lines 36–45, Ringler, pp. 234–5.   1. Ibid., p. 221.
2. Auden, ' "The Truest Poetry is the most Feigning" ', *Collected Shorter Poems
1927–1957*, p. 317. Many of the ideas in this poem are relevant to *Astrophil and Stella*.
3. Shepherd, p. 100.   4. e.g., *A.S.* 36, Ringler, p. 182.
5. e.g., *A.S.* 21, ibid., p. 175.   6. e.g., *A.S.* 28, ibid., p. 178.

The frequency with which poems are addressed to things which could not possibly read them—a highway,[7] a bed,[8] the Thames,[9] for instance—is a warning against too literal an interpretation. Then there is a kind of reader sometimes distinct, although not necessarily always, from those whom I have just mentioned. These are people who, being close friends of Sidney, might well be expected to read his poems—say Sidney's sister, Fulke Greville, and one or two others. Then I do not think that Sidney can have been entirely unaware that there was a world of potential readers outside his own circle, a world which his poems were likely to reach sooner or later, whether or not through the medium of print. There is a great gap between those readers and Sidney's close friends, but probably not so great a gap as there is between them and someone reading the poems now, nearly four hundred years after they were written and in a culture very remote from Sidney's.

In a sense we must be mainly concerned with the last kind of reader, since the value of Sidney's poetry to us is ultimately our reason for reading it at all. Nevertheless, if we want to understand it as it was meant to be understood—both in fairness to the author, and in fairness to ourselves since we are likely to gain more by seeing what he has to offer us than by attempting to cut such a fine poetic intelligence down to our own size—then we must try to understand something of the attitudes of the poems' first readers, those in the Sidney circle.

I have already discussed the nonchalant, aristocratic tone habitual with Sidney.[1] This involved the deliberate cultivation of a manner acceptable in the society in which he moved: '... fundamentally, the magnanimous man is also the courtly man. His virtue is not merely innate; it is self-conscious, deliberately cultivated in the midst of courts. It is more sophisticated and complex than mere brute courage.'[2] An unsympathetic way of putting it would be to say that such an attitude was not one it was necessary to *have* so much as one it was necessary to *strike*: an audience is presupposed. It could also be suggested that 'sophisticated' is only another word for 'affected', and that the audience

---

7. *A.S.* 84, ibid., p. 209. 8. *A.S.* 98, ibid., p. 230.
9. *A.S.* 103, ibid., p. 232. 1. Above, pp. 6–13.
2. Margaret Greaves, *The Blazon of Honour. A Study in Renaissance Magnanimity*, 1964, p. 29.

presupposed is one which puts a premium on frivolous and superficial attitudinizing. I think, however, that this would be unfair.

Certainly it was a small, intimate society, appreciative of private jokes and allusions, as the 'Rich' sonnets[3] suggest. It was also a society with elaborate conventions, in conduct as in writing; it is because the conventions are generally accepted that Astrophil's rejection of them here is dramatic:

> Because I breathe not love to everie one,
>   Nor do not use set colours for to weare,
>   Nor nourish speciall lockes of vowed haire,
>   Nor give each speech a full point of a grone,
>   The courtly Nymphs, acquainted with the mone
>   Of them, who in their lips *Love's* standerd beare;
>   'What he?' say they of me, 'now I dare sweare,
>   He cannot love; no, no, let him alone.'[4]

It would be quite wrong to regard either the acceptance or the rejection of the conventions as trivial affectation. To impose form, order, a set procedure on the expression of human feelings is not to deny them their deep significance, but rather to emphasize that they are human feelings and not merely animal ones; it marks a sense of the dignity of being a civilized being.[5] To play with the passions even, to display them in an apparently frivolous manner, is to show one's superiority to them, to dominate them rather than be dominated by them. Imposing this form upon the passions can therefore be regarded even as a moral duty.[6]

This is why it makes sense, and does not detract from the value of the poetry, to suggest that Sidney may well have prized his skill in tournament as highly as his skill in poetry.[7] Both were artistic accomplishments, one a civilizing of warfare and human aggression,[8] and the other a civilizing of human passions. We may now value the poetry more, and I certainly think we should; but it is arguable that to appreciate it properly we need to make an imaginative effort comparable to that of acquiring a taste for tournaments.

3. See above, pp. 63–5.   4. *A.S.* 54, Ringler, p. 191.
5. Evans, op. cit., p. 111.
6. L. G. Salingar, 'The Elizabethan Literary Renaissance', *A Guide to English Literature*, ed. Boris Ford, *The Age of Shakespeare*, 1955, ii, 94.
7. Buxton, *Sir Philip Sidney and the English Renaissance*, pp. 5–6.
8. See Yates, op. cit.

We must at the same time beware of imputing too limited an appeal to Sidney's sonnets: the great interest that is still taken in them would be enough to refute that. I am merely suggesting that, to some extent, we need to cultivate a taste. This description of what was involved in the vogue of sonneteering is clearly not a sympathetic one, but it does catch some of the atmosphere:

> . . . the Elizabethans admired individual aristocratic expertise—hawking, eloquence, sword-play, playing the lute. A sonnet is within the compass of most men and even an amateur sonnet is recognisable as an artifact. It also has magical value, as a token of existence and emotion, like the caskets, lockets, rings of the period. In its Elizabethan mode the sonnet is essentially a poem for giving; and to that extent it has often a cloacal air, of greed for the writer's own self, a bribe for favours, something to please you with. This makes sonnets stodgy to read outside the friendly circle they were first written for. . . .[9]

There are several statements here I will venture to disagree with. It is not easy to write a sonnet, even a middling one; but it is interesting that the Elizabethans so often give the impression that it is easy. That they were so expert in such a demanding form, one of the most artificial and restricted, tells us something of their interests and ideals. Then, is it true that sonnets, and 'caskets, lockets, rings', were used to stress that their owners existed? The dominant impression which remains with me after visiting the recent exhibition of Elizabethan painting at the Tate Gallery[1] is of people who did not need to prove to themselves that they existed, who were intensely aware of their own individuality, but who made use of a variety of accoutrements—such as elaborate clothing and jewels—to stress (what perhaps did need stressing to themselves) their civility and sophistication. The description of the Elizabethan sonnet as 'something to please you with' I find acceptable, and very relevant to Sidney's sonnets, without agreeing with the faint air of disapproval this phrase has in its context. Whether such sonnets are now 'stodgy to read' depends on how good they are of their kind. I should prefer to say, rather, of Sidney's at least, 'more difficult to read fairly' outside the circle for which they were first composed.

Another point needs touching on. Love, or its outward

9. Broadbent, op. cit., p. 73.

1. *The Elizabethan Image*, 28 November 1969–8 February 1970. See the catalogue of the same name by Roy Strong.

manifestations at least, was an obsession in this society. Spenser
mocks the obsession:

> . . . loue most aboundeth there.
> For all the walls and windows there are writ,
> All full of loue, and loue, and loue my deare,
> And all their talke and studie is of it.
> Ne any there doth braue or valiant seeme,
> Vnlesse that some gay Mistresse badge he beares:
> Ne any one himselfe doth ought esteeme,
> Vnlesse he swim in loue vp to the eares.[2]

Love and poetry were intimately connected with each other, as
Spenser the mocker shows as well as Sidney the mocker. It is
significant just how easily discussion of poetry in Sidney's *Apology*
turns into discussion of love.[3] That it was fashionable to seem in
love is one more reason for refusing to regard *Astrophil and Stella*
as necessarily the expression of Sidney's personal feelings. That it
was fashionable love which was fashionable, not simply affection
but rather the eloquent and stylized expression of something
called love, brings us right up against the question of how
seriously we are to take Astrophil's protestations. The banter and
parody of the lines I have just quoted from Spenser, which can
easily be matched in Sidney,[4] are part of the convention of courtly
poetry:[5] it was a convention that the conventions themselves
must not seem to be taken seriously always.

What I would argue against is any idea that we need to understand the conventions employed only in order to work through
them somehow to get at some simple feeling beneath. The manner
of expression is itself part of the experience each poem offers.
There may have been strong affection behind some of the poems,
and some of them certainly read like the expression of strong
affection,[6] but that is only one of many emotions expressed. To
regard it as essential seems to me to be very misleading:

In these sonnets we see, held still in time for us, a whole progress of
passion, physical and spiritual, coursing through rage and despair,

2. *Colin Clouts Come Home Againe*, lines 775–82, Spenser, p. 544.
3. Montgomery, p. 48; Rudenstine, p. 47.
4. e.g., *A.S.* 15, Ringler, p. 172.
5. Bradbrook, op. cit., p. 30.
6. e.g., *A.S.* 72, Song 11, Ringler, pp. 202, 233.

self-pity, hope renewed, exultancy, moon-moved dreams, black fear, and blinding bright certainty of final loss.[7]

Without denying that some of these feelings are to be found, I suggest that they are not the prominent ones. The prevalent manner of the sequence is witty and courtly, a manner suitable for complimentary verse. [8] Although it has often been recognized that some of the poems are *badinage* rather than expressions of amorous ardour,[9] it is still true that the poems as a whole tend to be taken too solemnly.[1] One of their hallmarks is their sophisticated good humour,[1] something, it must be stressed, well worth expressing.

A number of apparent difficulties arise if the reader is intent on following a 'progress of passion' in what is really complimentary verse. It has been said, for instance, that in these opening lines the 'personification is nearly ludicrous';[2]

Highway since you my chiefe *Pernassus* be . . . [3]

O happie Tems, that didst my *Stella* beare . . .[4]

And so it is, and intentionally so. Similarly, it has been objected that Sonnet 5, 'It is most true, that eyes are form'd to serve',[5] 'is a false syllogism, the conclusion standing in contradiction to the premisses'.[6] It is indeed, and it is meant to be: Sidney is joking.[7] The objection that the last lines of the poems are so often meant to startle that they usually fail to startle[8] also loses much of its force if we see the poems as complimentary ones. If, in some of the sonnets, 'Stella is introduced, somewhat obviously, to produce a full close',[9] this is far from detracting from the effectiveness of the poems as compliments. There is a certain pleasure in waiting

7. Thomas, op. cit., p. 120.

8. Jack Stillinger, 'The Biographical Problem of *Astrophel and Stella*', p. 637.

9. e.g., Michel Poirier, *Sir Philip Sidney*, p. 180.

1. Castley, op. cit., p. 65; Stillinger, 'The Biographical Problem of *Astrophel and Stella*', p. 634.

2. Montgomery, p. 90.   3. *A.S.* 84, Ringler, p. 209.

4. *A.S.* 103, ibid., p. 232.   5. Ibid., p. 167.

6. de Mourgues, op. cit., p. 14.

7. Castley, op. cit., pp. 57–8. See also above, pp. 70–1, and compare the manner in which Astrophil plays with the idea of the double negative in *A.S.* 63, Ringler, p. 196.

8. de Mourgues, op. cit., p. 129.

9. Prince, op. cit., p. 19, where the device is seen as justified since it occurs in some of Sidney's best poems, e.g., *A.S.* 41, 39, 84, 74, Ringler, pp. 185, 184, 209, 203.

to see how something apparently not to do with Stella will eventually be brought round to her.[1]

This may all seem like an elaborate game, and in a sense that is what it is—the game which Eric Berne calls 'Cavalier'.[2] In 'Cavalier' a man, who is not attempting seduction, tries to please a woman by displaying his skill in compliment. If the woman is willing to take part in the game, and sophisticated enough to play her part well, then it can become very elaborate:

A man of the world, of course, will know when to stop, and will not continue beyond the point at which he ceases to amuse (out of consideration for her) or where the quality of his offerings begins to deteriorate (out of consideration for his own pride of craftsmanship).[3]

Our difficulty in deciding always which poems in *Astrophil and Stella* are meant as compliments in this sort of game comes largely from our ignorance of how far it was acceptable to go in Sidney's circle, particularly with sexual innuendo. It is very likely that Stella would be pleased to find one sonnet ending with Astrophil deciding to

Pray that my sunne go downe with meeker beames to bed.[4]

It is possible, however, that this ending is a little too near the knuckle:

. . . while thy beautie drawes the heart to love,
As fast thy Vertue bends that love to good:
'But ah,' Desire still cries, 'give me some food.'[5]

I am inclined to think, mainly I suppose because of what I consider to be the dominant tone of the sequence, that this would be an acceptable compliment; but one cannot be sure.

There are further complications caused by the biographical intrusions into some of the poems. If some of them were meant, at least partly, as compliments to Penelope Rich then the game becomes very complex, since the compliments come under the guise of poems written by Astrophil for Stella, with only a hint of Sidney and Penelope. In this game what the poet 'is offering for

1. e.g., *A.S.* 5, 15, 21, 23, 26, ibid., pp. 167, 172, 175, 176, 177. See also above, p. 116.
2. *Games People Play: The Psychology of Human Relationships*, 1968, pp. 144–5.
3. Ibid., p. 144.   4. *A.S.* 76, Ringler, p. 205.   5. *A.S.* 71, ibid., p. 201.

appreciation is not himself, but his poetry',[6] and we do not know how appreciative Penelope was of poetry, or how inclined she might have been to take the game too seriously.

What is offered is something more valuable than the expression of passion—a civilized way of looking at things. A frequent ingredient in this is a touch of humour, not to destroy the effect of the compliment, but rather to strengthen it. These lines are certainly complimentary:

> Soule's joy, bend not those morning starres from me,
>   Where Vertue is made strong by Beautie's might,
>   Where *Love* is chastnesse, Paine doth learne delight,
> And Humblenesse growes one with Majestie.[7]

Part of the value of any compliment, however, depends on the recipient's being persuaded that it is offered by a good judge, someone who knows what he is talking about. The end of this poem is, for that very reason, more effective than the beginning;[8] Astrophil is speaking of Stella's eyes:

> . . . though I oft my selfe of them bemone,
>   That through my heart their beamie darts be gone,
> Whose curelesse wounds even now most freshly bleed:
>   Yet since my death-wound is already got,
>   Deare Killer, spare not thy sweet cruell shot:
> A kind of grace it is to slay with speed.[9]

There is a comic gap between what Astrophil is asking for and the image used to express it; after all, he is only asking for a glance.[1] The hyperbole attains just the right tone, laudatory but not mawkish. Who would not be pleased to receive a compliment from such a subtle, balanced, and discriminating mind as this sonnet reveals?

Those for whom the compliment was not primarily intended may still enjoy the poem. In asking implicitly that we be alive to various subtleties, including the exact relation between a concept and the image used to express it,[2] *Astrophil and Stella* in a sense compliments anyone who reads it. If we need to try to recapture something of the society in which these poems were written in

6. Berne, op. cit., p. 145.   7. *A.S.* 48, Ringler, p. 188.
8. See above, p. 36.   9. *A.S.* 48, Ringler, p. 189.
1. Myrick, op. cit., p. 310.   2. See above, pp. 30-3.

order to appreciate them, it is also true that the best way of recapturing some of that vanished civility is by reading the poems. Passion there may be in some of them, passion there may have been behind all of them for all we know, but we, as lookers-on after four centuries, go to them for pleasure, the pleasure of graceful expression, and I think it answers their intention very well if 'pastime, not passion enters'[3] into our minds when we read them.

3. *O.A.* 13, line 41, Ringler, p. 32.

4

A feeling skill[1]

ONE OF THE FASCINATIONS of any sonnet-sequence is the pull
between our inclination to read each sonnet as a self-contained
poem and our knowledge that it is also part of a larger whole. To
revert to the metaphor of *Astrophil and Stella* as a play—each
sonnet has its own distinctive personality, and this personality
interacts with the personalities of the other sonnets. Such a comment as this is particularly relevant to *Astrophil and Stella*: 'Every
sonnet is a compressed drama, and every sonnet-sequence is a
greater drama built up of such dramatic moments.'[2] Since I have
discussed some sonnets, or parts of them, with reference to the
main question of how we should read the drama as a whole, I shall
in this chapter discuss in a little detail some of the 'dramatic
moments'. I shall choose among those which seem to me to be
most successful and (a further indication of the generally high
standard maintained in the sequence) they will be sonnets which
I have more or less neglected up to now.

The dramatic qualities of individual sonnets are evident even in
comparatively small matters of technique. The frequent contrast
between an elaborate tissue of figures and a simple, often collo-
quial, diction[3] is dramatic. The beginning of the first sonnet is
typical:

Loving in truth, and faine in verse my love to show,
That the deare She might take some pleasure of my paine:
Pleasure might cause her reade, reading might make her know,
Knowledge might pitie winne, and pitie grace obtaine,
    I sought fit words to paint the blackest face of woe . . .[4]

1. *A.S.* 2, Ringler, p. 166.   2. Prince, op. cit., p. 20.
3. Robertson, 'Sir Philip Sidney and his Poetry', p. 128.
4. Ringler, p. 165.

Here we may notice the use of alliteration, personification, and metaphor, all combined in the main figure of climax (a more complex figure than appears from these few lines, since this climax is only one of several in the poem all leading up to the main climax at the end); and we may notice too the simplicity of the diction in contrast to the complexity of the figures. This contrast is one reason why the poems in *Astrophil and Stella* seem so often to be both highly wrought and artless at the same time. The ending of the second sonnet may look at first like simplicity itself; certainly the diction is simple:

> . . . And now employ the remnant of my wit,
> To make my selfe beleeve, that all is well,
> While with a feeling skill I paint my hell.[5]

If we wished for an instance of a 'natural style', the concluding couplet might well come to mind; but on a careful reading we are bound to become aware of the artifice which has gone into its making, if only when we notice that the full rhyme of 'well' and 'hell' is combined with half-rhymes made by 'all' and 'skill'.[6] These half-rhymes have the effect of muting what would otherwise be a strong rhyme at the ends of the lines; the statement 'all is well', strong in itself, is qualified by the preceding 'To make my selfe beleeve'; and the last line is slowed down by the parenthetical 'with a feeling skill': these details work against the natural tendency of the couplet to seem self-confident. We gather what Astrophil means by 'the remnant of my wit', and we are glad to find that 'the remnant' is sufficient to ensure the adequate expression of his plight.

As with diction and figures, so with metre. Any writer of poetry in English is, and any reader of poetry in English ought to be, aware of the constant tug between the regular pattern of the metre and the variations caused by the speech-stress, the stress demanded by the sense and tone of the lines.[7] Many things go to make up the total effect which we call 'rhythm'; but this dramatic conflict of stresses is arguably the most important. It is part of the tension there always is between a poem as a sort of ritual celebration, a well-proportioned artefact, and a poem as something that seems

5. *A.S.* 2, ibid., p. 166.   6. Rudenstine, p. 192.
7. There is an interesting discussion of this matter in Martin Halpern, 'On the Two Chief Metrical Modes in English', *P.M.L.A.* lxxvii (1962), 177–86.

the natural, inevitable expression of human notions and feelings. These lines, for instance, are perfectly metrical, and to that extent are formal and even ritualistic:

> It is most true, that eyes are form'd to serve
> The inward light: and that the heav'nly part
> Ought to be king, from whose rules who do swerve,
> Rebels to Nature, strive for their owne smart.[8]

The inversion of the first foot in the third line, where 'Ought' takes a stress instead of 'to', is an example of a practice very common in English verse, a practice which we may call 'allowable' in the sense that it is something poets may do while still preserving the feel of a metrical pattern. It is worth mentioning, however, that such devices, now part of any poet's equipment, were not always so obvious: Sidney's metrical skill has some historical importance. One need only read Gascoigne to notice a difference:[9]

> My woorthy Lord, I pray you wonder not,
> To see your woodman shoote so ofte awrie,
> Nor that he stands amased like a sot,
> And lets the harmlesse deare (unhurt) go by.[1]

These are not lines which I would wish to denigrate, and there are signs of something metrically very interesting at the beginning of the third line; but Gascoigne's regularity is comparatively uncomplicated, with the metrical and speech stresses tending to coincide, and this is evidence of a lack of certainty about metre which is noticeable generally in English poets before Sidney and Spenser. However, Sidney's historical importance, as one of the first to exploit fully a quality of English verse which now seems obvious, is not what I am mainly concerned with here. It is the subtly dramatic use he makes of it which matters. He could, of course, have ensured a stress on 'Ought' by placing it in a position where it would take a metrical stress. But, by stressing it in conflict with the metrical pattern, he stresses it more;[2] this is important in a poem whose theme is the distinction between what ought

8. *A.S.* 5, Ringler, p. 167.
9. Thompson, *The Founding of English Metre*, p. 152.
1. Gascoigne, ed. cit., 'Gascoignes woodmanship', i, 348.
2. Thompson, *The Founding of English Metre*, p. 151.

to be and what is; the extra weight on 'Ought' is a hint of what to expect later in the poem, what is stated directly in the very last line:

True, and yet true that I must *Stella* love.[3]

Such metrical dexterity is normal in *Astrophil and Stella*.

To say that some of the sonnets in *Astrophil and Stella* are better than others is only to say what might safely be hazarded by someone who had never read the sequence. I shall concentrate on some of Sidney's successes, partly because the proportion of them is very high, and partly because, with such a fine poet, effort is better spent in attempting to appreciate the subtlety of his effects than in picking out faults. Nevertheless, it would be misleading to imply that the writing in *Astrophil and Stella* is faultless:

There is so much careless writing in *Astrophel and Stella* that malicious quotation could easily make it appear a failure. Sidney can hiss like a serpent ('Sweet swelling lips well maist thou swell'), gobble like a turkey ('Moddels such be wood globes'), and quack like a duck ('But God wot, wot not what they mean').[4]

The main point here is sound, and the examples given speak (or 'hiss' or 'gobble') for themselves. But some caution is necessary. Certainly the last words Lewis quotes do 'quack like a duck'; but it is arguable that they are meant to: in their context, where the tone is one of mock-solemnity,[5] their ludicrous sound is dramatically appropriate:

Some do I hear of Poets' furie tell,
But (God wot) wot not what they meane by it:
And this I swear by blackest brooke of hell,
I am no pick-purse of another's wit.[6]

Similarly, the tongue-twisting nature of a line worse than any quoted by Lewis may be a way of stressing the difficulties faced by 'Reason', who is addressed in the poem:

Why shouldst thou toyle our thornie soile to till?[7]

3. *A.S.* 5, Ringler, p. 167.
4. Lewis, *English Literature in the Sixteenth Century*, 329.
5. See above, pp. 19–20.   6. *A.S.* 74, Ringler, p. 204.
7. *A.S.* 10, ibid., p. 169.

In contrast, it is easy to pick out harmonious lines:

> And in her eyes of arrowes infinit.[8]

> No lovely *Paris* made thy *Hellen* his . . .[9]

> O do not let thy Temple be destroyd.[1]

In general, however, it is not mellifluence which we can expect, so much as a dramatic appropriateness of the sound and rhythm:

> Vertue awake, Beautie but beautie is,
> I may, I must, I can, I will, I do
> Leave following that, which it is gaine to misse.
> Let her go. Soft, but here she comes. Go to,
> Unkind, I love you not: O me, that eye
> Doth make my heart give to my tongue the lie.[2]

Another problem in *Astrophil and Stella* is the frequent inversion of word-order. Often this is justified by the emphasis it gives (we still use inversion in speech for this effect):

> His mother deare *Cupid* offended late . . .[3]

At other times it helps to give that sense of formality, even ritual, which all poetry must have, and which is particularly needed on some occasions:

> Muses, I oft invoked your holy ayde,
> With choisest flowers my speech to engarland so;
> That it, despisde in true but naked shew,
> Might winne some grace in your sweet skill arraid.[4]

Sometimes, I must admit, it is simply a nuisance;[5] it seems to be only a way (convenient to Sidney, but not to his reader) of coping with the demands of rhyme or metre:

> Who hath the voyce, which soule from sences sunders,
> Whose force but yours the bolts of beautie thunders?
> To you, to you, all song of praise is due:
> Only with you not miracles are wonders.[6]

8. *A.S.* 17, ibid., p. 173.   9. *A.S.* 33, ibid., p. 181.
1. *A.S.* 40, ibid., p. 185.   2. *A.S.* 47, ibid., p. 188.
3. *A.S.* 17, ibid., p. 173.   4. *A.S.* 55, ibid., p. 192.
5. See above, p. 68, on *C.S.* 5.   6. Song 1, lines 29–32, Ringler, p. 197.

The inversions in the first and second lines are rhetorically justified, since they throw the weight of emphasis on the powerful
verbs 'sunders' and 'thunders'; the inversion in the third line also
puts the emphasis where it is needed, on 'To you, to you'; but
there seems to be an inversion in the fourth line caused by the
demands of metre and possibly by the need for a rhyme, and it
results in an unfortunate ambiguity. The line may mean 'Only
with you miracles are not wonders';[7] it may mean 'Only with
you wonders are not miracles';[8] or it may mean 'Only with you
things that are not miracles are wonders'. The last is possibly the
strongest and most appropriate sense, and it does not involve an
inversion. It does, however, involve a rather strange form of expression, and our doubt as to the meaning of the line is a weakness
in the poem. On the other hand, there are occasions when inversion results in a fruitful ambiguity.[9]

In reading any poem in *Astrophil and Stella* we must be alive to
all sorts of ingenuity. I do not mean that we should look for any
possible meaning a word could have: Sidney's ambiguities are
normally precise and their presence is indicated by the context
within which the various meanings co-operate. The play on
'touch' in Sonnet 9 is a case in point;[1] meanings are multiplied, but
in a lucid, if difficult, way, and the meanings are not such as to
cancel each other out: Sidney is sure of his touch. I do not think
that Sidney ever intends us to go off at a tangent to pursue any
possible meanings his words may have; he wants us to be alive
to the mutually supporting meanings which the context suggests.
A line from one of the *Certain Sonnets* may illustrate the point; the
poem is about desire:

Thou blind man's marke, thou foole's selfe chosen snare . . .[2]

The meaning of 'marke' here is 'target';[3] but one critic, after recog-
nizing this, says: 'But desire is the blind man's mark also because
it marks him, like the patch over his eyes.'[4] The difficulty is that
the notions of 'target' and 'sign' are mutually exclusive: I do not
think that anyone can read both meanings at once. One might just
as well argue that 'marke' suggests a sum of money, and so desire

7. Ibid., p. 479. 8. Gentili, p. 367.
9. See below, p. 151. 1. See above, pp. 5–6.
2. *C.S.* 31, Ringler, p. 161. 3. Ibid., p. 434.
4. Hoffman, 'Sidney's *Thou blind man's mark*', *Explicator*, viii (1949–50), Article 29.

is the sole wealth of one who cannot see what other wealth there is, and so on, and so on. If Sidney had wanted the ambiguity which Hoffman suggests, he would have shown he wanted it, and also fitted the extra meaning into the poem so that it worked with, and not against, the obvious one: many poems demonstrate his ability to do this.

Sonnet 39, 'Come sleepe, ô sleepe, the certaine knot of peace',[5] has (very appropriately for a poem addressed to sleep) an almost hypnotic effect:

> Come sleepe, ô sleepe, the certaine knot of peace,
> The baiting place of wit, the balme of woe,
> The poore man's wealth, the prisoner's release,
> Th'indifferent Judge betweene the high and low;
>   With shield of proofe shield me from out the prease
> Of those fierce darts, dispaire at me doth throw:
> O make me in those civill warres to cease;
> I will good tribute pay if thou do so.

Even the smallest details of the sound here are beautifully controlled:

The nice variation of vowel sounds; the subtle alliteration of p, l, s, in the octave, binding the lines and quatrains together, yet interrupted in the sixth line (because of its content) by the hard dentals; the cross-alliteration in the second line (bwbw): these are some of the indications of the poet's craftsmanship.[6]

These details are supported by conscious rhetoric on a larger scale: the second and third lines both contain a pair of metaphors for sleep, and so are balanced within themselves and with each other, and they are rounded off by a fourth line made up of only one metaphor.[7] This does not exhaust the artistry of the first four lines. The second and third lines are balanced not only in the way I have just mentioned. They are also related in a sort of syllabic chiasmus, since line 2 is made up of six syllables plus four syllables, and line 3 of four syllables plus six syllables. There is also a grammatical contrast, in the different forms used to show possession, between the two lines. The casual, throw-away manner of the eighth line is surprising in its context and contrasts dramatically

---

5. Ringler, p. 184.   6. Muir, *Sir Philip Sidney*, p. 34.
7. Buxton, *Elizabethan Taste*, p. 284.

with the stateliness of the poem's opening,[8] a stateliness to which the rhetorical complexity I have described contributes. The poem reaches a preliminary climax in this eighth line with its promise of tribute; the line also creates further suspense, since we are waiting to hear what the tribute will be;[9] the main climax comes, as so often, at the very end of the poem, when we are told that the greatest tribute offered is '*Stella's* image'.

The first eight lines are mainly an assembly of images used to build up an idea of the nature and desirability of sleep, and the last six lines balance them with a catalogue of the various kinds of tribute offered:

> Take thou of me smooth pillowes, sweetest bed,
> A chamber deafe to noise, and blind to light:
> A rosie garland, and a wearie hed:
> And if these things, as being thine by right,
>   Move not thy heavy grace, thou shalt in me,
>   Livelier then else-where, *Stella's* image see.

The adjective in 'sweetest bed' may seem rather vague and weak, until we remember that this word was often used of scents; probably the reference is to scented sheets.[1] With its touch of formality, 'rosie garland' contrasts with the homeliness of 'smooth pillowes'. The garland is not merely decorative; it is emblematic of silence and secrecy, as in the proverbial phrase '*sub rosa*';[2] and the origin of this emblem is appropriately recalled in this poem on love and sleep; the rose was dedicated to the god of silence, Harpocrates, by Cupid in return for help in Venus' intrigues.[3] Vanna Gentili has pointed out[4] the subtlety in the apparently simple phrase 'thy heavy grace'. This is both a form of address to sleep and also a reference to the favour hoped for from sleep. In addition, the word 'grace' can denote a quality, and the adjective 'heavy', by its unexpectedness, suggests this further sense: we usually think of gracefulness as something light and delicate. The adjective 'heavy' is unexpected, and yet it is clearly accurate: sleep's 'grace', whether as a polite form of address, or as a favour, or as a quality, must be 'heavy' because of the torpor associated with sleep.

All these details are controlled by the main strategy of the

8. Ibid., p. 285.   9. Ibid., p. 284.   1. Ibid., pp. 284–5.
2. Ibid., p. 285.   3. Ringler, p. 473.   4. Gentili, p. 312.

poem, a strategy of which Sidney is very fond.[5] We expect the
poem to be about Stella, but it is only in the last line that the poem
is explicitly brought round to her. All the previous poems of the
sequence, and particularly the one immediately preceding,[6] and
hints in this poem itself (the 'civill warres'[7] and the 'rosie garland') have led us to expect this ending, which still comes as a
surprise, largely I think because of the shock of the word 'Live-
lier' in a poem so evocative of sleep. The last line draws together
various strands in the poem: it satisfies us by taking us where we
thought we must be going—to Stella; it answers the question
which everything has tacitly encouraged us to ask—Why is he
awake? and it brings the offers of tribute to a climax, and so
compliments Stella.

Sonnet 39, while perhaps more musical than most, is still in a
manner familiar from many other sonnets in *Astrophil and Stella*;
but Sonnet 103, 'O happie Tems, that didst my *Stella* beare',[8]
comes as something of a surprise. It is comparatively undramatic,
lacking conflict[9] except for the simple 'faire disgrace' of Stella's
dishevelment, and rather reminiscent of the more stately and
straightforward sonnets of Spenser's *Amoretti*.[1] The poem is
pictorial, in a special way:

> O happie Tems, that didst my *Stella* beare,
> I saw thy selfe with many a smiling line
> Upon thy cheerefull face, joye's livery weare:
> While those faire planets on thy streames did shine.

This is a picture in the sense in which Sidney uses the word in his
Apology: 'Poesy therefore is an art of imitation, for so Aristotle
termeth it in his word *mimesis*, that is to say, a representing,
counterfeiting, or figuring forth—to speak metaphorically, a
speaking picture—with this end, to teach and delight.'[2] Sidney
makes it clear he does not mean anything like what we call a
photographic representation; this is particularly obvious in his
comparison of his 'right poets' with a painter who paints qualities
like 'the constant though lamenting look of Lucretia, when she
punished in herself another's fault; wherein he painteth not Lucretia

5. See above, pp. 116, 132-3.   6. *A.S.* 38, Ringler, p. 183.
7. See above, p. 117.   8. Ringler, p. 232.
9. Gentili, p. 489.   1. Spenser, p. 561.
2. Shepherd, p. 101.

whom he never saw, but painteth the outward beauty of such a virtue'.[3] This poem is 'a speaking picture' of Astrophil's joy; and the half-comic unreality of his addressing a river,[4] and his cheerful attribution to the river of his own joy, are appropriate to his mood.

The inversion in line 5, 'The bote for joy could not to daunce forbeare', is a means of representing rhythmically the movement of the boat which is itself mentioned only because it is a picture of joy. The 'wanton winds' which twine themselves in Stella's hair are also mentioned not for the sake of naturalistic description but as a means of embodying Astrophil's own feelings. The winds are not at first visualized at all sharply:

> . . . While wanton winds with beauties so devine
> Ravisht, staid not, till in her golden haire
> They did themselves (ô sweetest prison) twine.

When we are encouraged to visualize them, immediately afterwards, it is as emblematic figures:

> And faine those *Aeols*' youthes there would their stay
> Have made, but forst by Nature still to flie,
> First did with puffing kisse those lockes display . . .

They bring to mind the representation of the winds in Botticelli's *Birth of Venus*, and one cannot help wondering whether Sidney had seen this painting.[5] Botticelli has a pair of '*Aeols*' youthes' puffing their cheeks to blow Venus' hair into charming disorder as she floats to land on a shell, and there is a joyful, springlike quality, and 'a lucid elegance'[6] in both works. If, as has been suggested, the painting shows 'the dual nature of love, both sensuous and chaste',[7] then that is a further similarity to the poem where Stella is ashamed to be 'discheveld' and yet still worthy of the highest honour:

> . . . She so discheveld, blusht; from window I
> With sight thereof cride out; ô faire disgrace,
> Let honor' selfe to thee graunt highest place.

Of course the Thames, however 'happie', makes a background very different from the stylized and unspecified sea of the *Birth of*

3. Shepherd, p. 102.   4. See above, p. 132.   5. Gentili, p. 489.
6. Wind, *Pagan Mysteries in the Renaissance*, 1967, p. 132.   7. Ibid., p. 131.

Venus. In the poem the situation is mythologized in a contemporary setting. The same thing happens, with a comic effect, in Sonnet 20, 'Flie, fly, my friends, I have my death wound; fly'.[8] Astrophil announces his death at the hands of a footpad; while enjoying the view he has been shot from the ambush of a 'darke bush' by a 'bloudie bullet'; he is ending up as many Elizabethans must have done. But the footpad has started his career young, he is a 'murthring boy', and turns out in fact to be Astrophil's usual antagonist Cupid, completely identified near the end of the poem by 'the glistring of his dart'. The change from 'bullet' to 'dart' is, I think, intentional: the modern and the obsolescent are mingled[9] so that we have strongly presented to us both the sense of a particular situation and the universal significance of that situation. Although I think it is intentional, I am still not quite happy about this mixture; however, it is a relief to be sure that 'bullet' can here be taken in its modern sense of a small missile,[1] and that we do not have to imagine a footpad firing cannon-balls.

The comic effect of the poem comes mainly from the disproportion between its theme—Astrophil has been looked at by Stella—and the imagery used to convey this.[2] Details in the poem support this effect of comedy, and the poem is a good instance of witty compliment, all the more complimentary for being witty. The 'darke bush' in which Cupid lies in wait is Stella's black eyes, and

> Poore passenger, passe now thereby I did,
> And staid pleasd with the prospect of the place,
> While that black hue from me the bad guest hid . . .

Astrophil's blissful ignorance just before he is hit is that of the clown moving into position for the custard-pie, and the inversion of word-order in the first line, 'Poore passenger, passe now thereby I did,' gives just the impression of pomposity needed for the coming disaster to seem most funny. None of this is to deny that the ending of the poem seems serious:

> . . . straight I saw motions of lightning' grace,
> And then descried the glistring of his dart:
> But ere I could flie thence, it pierc'd my heart.

8. Ringler, p. 174.   9. Gentili, p. 260.   1. Ibid., p. 261.
2. See above, p. 134, on *A.S.* 48.

The poem is intended seriously enough in one sense, as a compliment.

As I have already suggested,[3] a compliment is all the more effective when it is offered by one who is patently intelligent and witty. Sonnet 59 ,'Deare, why make you more of a dog then me?'[4] comes to a climax in Astrophil's acceptance of all the demands of love, even if they include the loss of that very wit which the poem has demonstrated to be so fertile and subtle:[5]

> Alas, if you grant only such delight
> To witlesse things, then *Love* I hope (since wit
> Becomes a clog) will soone ease me of it.

This is partly a last fling in the attempt to strike some response from Stella, and partly a veiled threat to her that the compliments may stop. The poem as a whole is a series of highly ingenious arguments to prove that Astrophil is—and this is the most comic thing of all—worth more than a dog. We have therefore the dramatic paradox that Astrophil is ludicrous in his humility and admirable for his wit. The arguments are not only consistently clever, but also subtly varied in their emotional impact. Astrophil can be ardent:

> Deare, why make you more of a dog then me?
> If he do love, I burne, I burne in love . . .

Much of the effect here comes from the contrast in the rhythm of the lines: the first is only just metrical, and it plods along with but one slight break (after the first word), while the second has a heavily emphasized metre, moves quickly, and is broken twice so that the effect is of sudden, sharp, deeply felt exclamations. Almost immediately afterwards Astrophil adopts a coaxing tone:

> If he be faire, yet but a dog can be.

The implication here is that Astrophil is suggesting what any reasonable person would see to be true. In the very next line the tone changes to one of scorn:

> Litle he is, so litle worth is he . . .

Yet in one way the scorn rebounds on Astrophil, who is reduced to being scornful of a dog. The comparison of a lover to a dog was

3. Above, p. 134.   4. Ringler, p. 194.
5. Gentili, p. 355; Kalstone, p. 160.

147

a poetical commonplace;[6] the effectiveness of it in this poem does not lie only in the 'turn of wit at the end',[7] fine though this is, but in the striking of a number of different right tones; the comparison is never given any more seriousness than it can bear. Once again we have a comic poem intended seriously, as a compliment.

Sonnet 75, 'Of all the kings that ever here did raigne',[8] is one of those poems which begin apparently far away from Stella, only to reach her at the very end. Many of the effects in *Astrophil and Stella* are repeated, but usually with some variation. This poem reaches Stella only implicitly: it is an oblique indication of Astrophil's own attitude to Stella when Edward IV is praised because he

> durst prove
> To lose his Crowne, rather then faile his Love.

The poem is deliberately shocking. It catalogues praiseworthy qualities, especially military skill and statesmanship, which it says Edward possessed, so that he seems an outstanding example of 'virtue',[9] and then it disparages these qualities:

> Of all the kings that ever here did raigne,
> *Edward* named fourth, as first in praise I name,
> Not for his faire outside, nor well lined braine,
> Although lesse gifts impe feathers oft on Fame,
>   Nor that he could young-wise, wise-valiant frame
> His Sire's revenge, joyn'd with a kingdome's gaine:
> And gain'd by *Mars*, could yet mad *Mars* so tame,
> That Ballance weigh'd what sword did late obtaine,
>   Nor that he made the Flouredeluce so fraid,
> Though strongly hedg'd of bloudy Lyon's pawes,
> That wittie *Lewis* to him a tribute paid.
> Nor this, nor that, nor any such small cause . . .

These lines show Sidney's characteristic weaknesses as well as some of his strengths. The sound of the fourth line is not very satisfactory: it would be an exaggeration to call it cacophonous, but it is undistinguished in sound except for the f's and s's, which make it rather hard to read. In contrast the seventh line has a powerful sound which reinforces the sense:

> And gain'd by *Mars*, could yet mad *Mars* so tame . . .

6. Ringler, pp. 477–8.   7. Ibid., p. 478.   8. Ibid., p. 204.
9. See above, pp. 75–6.

The alliteration on m draws attention to Mars and to the change in the attitude to war which the adjective 'mad' brings about. The verbs 'gain'd' and 'tame' are placed so as to stand out and contrast with each other. The structure of the line is itself an example of the wise subordination of means to ends for which Edward is said to be famous. There is a similar strength in this line:

> That Ballance weigh'd what sword did late obtaine . . .

The line is thoughtfully poised, with 'Ballance' against 'sword' and 'weigh'd' against 'obtaine', in imitation of the consideration in Edward's mind.

There are other faults in the sound of the poem. The first eight lines are rhymed ABABBABA; but the similarity of the nasals in all the rhyme-words causes much of the distinction between the A-rhymes and the B-rhymes to be lost, so that we have the impression of an unsuccessful attempt at monorhyme. In contrast to this, the strategy of the poem is highly successful: discussion of a historical figure is brought to bear on Astrophil's personal situation, while this discussion has also its own value as political comment. Further, the poem is rather more shocking than I have so far shown. It is not simply that Edward is praised for his love rather than his statesmanship: most of the poem is devoted to stressing the statesmanship of a king who was more renowned for unscrupulous political manoeuvring and self-indulgence.[1]

There is, if anything, an even more patent sophistry in Sonnet 63, 'O Grammer rules, ô now your vertues show',[2] where Astrophil seizes on Stella's twice saying no to him to argue

> That in one speech two Negatives affirme.

Even if we read the poem with modern usage in mind, it is clear that Astrophil is indulging in sophistry, since Stella's intention was obvious; but in Sidney's day, when the double negative was a customary form of emphasis, without an affirmative effect, then the sophistry would be even greater, since Astrophil's 'Grammer rules' are those of Latin and not of English.[3] It would be a misreading to object that, since the argument is false, Stella would be unlikely to be persuaded by it. Seduction by sophistry is not the

---

1. Ringler, p. 481.   2. Ibid., p. 196.   3. Ibid., p. 478.

intention. The whole point of the poem lies in the fact, obvious although never stated directly, that Astrophil is trying to persuade himself of the opposite of what Stella meant. The 'high triumphing' of the poem is only on the surface, a cover for an underlying sadness. Astrophil knows that he is trying to deceive himself: he admits that Stella said no twice 'Least once should not be heard.' We have again the paradox that Astrophil seems ridiculous in his attempted self-deception and also masterful and in command of the situation because of the wit which reveals he knows where he stands. If there is an epithalamic suggestion in the shout of triumph 'Io Pean',[4] then this is a further touch of wit: there can be no question of a marriage between Stella and Astrophil whose intentions are far less honourable.

Sonnet 69, 'O joy, too high for my low stile to show',[5] is another poem in which apparent joy partly conceals real sadness. Stella has now given her heart to Astrophil, but on a condition that detracts from much of the pleasure of this: he must take a 'vertuous course'. The shout of triumph in Sonnet 63, 'Io Pean', is subtly recalled here:

> I, I, ô I may say, that she is mine.[6]

This shows once more how the poems gain when read together, and it stresses what a careful reading the poems require. The effect is important—Astrophil is shown in artistic command of a situation he finds distressing—and yet it may easily go unnoticed. It practically disappears from a modernized text:

> I, I, oh I may say that she is mine.[7]

Like the sonnet on Edward IV, this poem uses political ideas for the expression of love, and, although the expression of love is the

4. Young, p. 61; but see Ringler, p. 478. The use of 'io Paean' was not restricted to marriage celebrations, and for them a more precise exclamation was 'io Hymen' (see Spenser's *Epithalamion*, line 140, Spenser, p. 581). Nevertheless, we can easily see that 'io Hymen' would have been obviously unfitting in this context, whereas 'Io Pean' may well contain an ironic hint of marriage.

5. Ringler, p. 200.

6. Young, p. 63; Evans, op. cit., p. 104: 'There is superb irony in the way Sidney makes Astrophil's exultant cry suggest the Io, Io of the traditional marriage song, at the moment when he is protesting the purely spiritual nature of his love.'

7. Craik, op. cit., p. 59.

dominant intention, the political ideas are also interesting in their own right:

> . . . though she give but thus conditionly
> This realme of blisse, while vertuous course I take,
> No kings be crown'd but they some covenants make.

Sonnet 69 is addressed to a friend 'that oft saw through all maskes my wo', and the mask in that poem is the political image. An earlier sonnet uses a different mask, one often employed in *Astrophil and Stella*, that of literary discussion:

> *Stella* oft sees the verie face of wo
>> Painted in my beclowded stormie face:
>> But cannot skill to pitie my disgrace,
> Not though thereof the cause her selfe she know:
> Yet hearing late a fable, which did show
>> Of Lovers never knowne, a grievous case,
>> Pitie thereof gate in her breast such place
> That, from that sea deriv'd, teares' spring did flow.
>> Alas, if Fancy drawne by imag'd things,
> Though false, yet with free scope more grace doth breed
> Then servant's wracke, where new doubts honor brings;
> Then thinke my deare, that you in me do reed
>> Of Lover's ruine some sad Tragedie:
>> I am not I, pitie the tale of me.[8]

Some incidental felicities may be mentioned briefly. The ambiguity in the fourth line is justified[9] because both possible meanings are relevant: 'even though she herself knows what the cause of my woe is', and 'even though she knows that she herself is the cause of my woe'.[1] Line 11 contains a similar relevant ambiguity in 'where new doubts honor brings'. 'Doubts' means 'qualms' or 'scruples'.[2] The primary sense is that Stella's sense of honour, her chastity, makes her all the more scrupulous in the face of Astrophil's distress. There is also a secondary meaning, or implication, that the scruples bring her honour; and this meaning is critical of her, since her honour depends on Astrophil's distress. The wit and playfulness of the poem's ending should not be lost,[3]

8. *A.S.* 45, Ringler, p. 187.
1. Ibid., pp. 474–5; Gentili, p. 326.
3. Myrick, op. cit., p. 312.

9. But see ibid., p. 474.
2. Ibid.

particularly since, when Astrophil says 'I am not I', we are led to consider who he might be, and his literary ideas here are exactly those of Sir Philip Sidney.

The sonnet is both a complaint of Stella's cruelty and a piece of critical theory. It has been argued that, although the literary discussion is proposed as a means of discussing the love situation, the emphasis in this poem is such as to make the love situation really a way of talking about literature.[4] I should not wish to go quite so far: the manifest absurdity of the suggestion in the last line makes me think that the love situation is as important here as elsewhere in the sequence. As in other sonnets,[5] Astrophil manages to cover both subjects at once. The literary theory involved is that poetry may move us when reality does not. In his *Apology* Sidney puts it like this:[6]

. . . how much it can move, Plutarch yieldeth a notable testimony of the abominable tyrant Alexander Pheraeus, from whose eyes a tragedy, well made and represented, drew abundance of tears, who without all pity had murdered infinite numbers, and some of his own blood; so as he that was not ashamed to make matters for tragedies, yet could not resist the sweet violence of a tragedy.[7]

There is, in the sonnet, a comic disproportion between the 'sad Tragedie' of which Astrophil says he wants Stella to think and its analogue in Astrophil's real life (which, to complicate matters further, is an artistic creation itself): the tone of the last three lines is such as to preclude our taking the 'Tragedie' too seriously. As so often, passion disappears behind the ingenuity which makes the poem a compliment.

In that poem Astrophil is, as usual, very conscious of the part he has chosen to play. This typically Elizabethan zest in the role of the moment continually makes it hard, if not impossible, for us to assess the exact nature of Astrophil's love (not to mention Sidney's feelings which were presumably involved somehow) in any other terms than those which the poems use. I think it helps, however,

4. Gentili, pp. 324–5.
5. e.g., *A.S.* 15, Ringler, p. 172.
6. The relation between this poem and the *Apology* is stressed in T. B. Stroup, 'The "Speaking Picture" Realised: Sidney's 45th Sonnet', *P.Q.* xxix (1950), 440–2.
7. Shepherd, p. 118.

to suggest that Astrophil would have appreciated what Yeats meant when he said:

> O what am I that I should not seem
> For the song's sake a fool?[8]

Sidney certainly saw no reason why he should not make Astrophil seem a fool and at the same time a skilled artist, and both for the song's sake. Astrophil's sophistication (a reflection of course of the sophistication of his creator) must be matched by a sophisticated reading. A sophisticated reading demands a constant awareness of the poems as artefacts, human fabrications which could have been different. One of the greatest pleasures of Sidney's poetic masterpiece is missed if we are not always alive, not only to the effects created, but also to the ways in which they are created. This kind of response, which Sidney could expect of his contemporary audience,[9] is the kind of response which Spenser encourages us to give to the picture of Leda in the House of Busyrane:

> O wondrous skill, and sweet wit of the man,
> That her in daffadillies sleeping made . . .[1]

However we look at it, *Astrophil and Stella* presents us with paradoxes. Astrophil talks much of his misery, and yet his conversation is a joy to listen to; the poems are witty, elaborately wrought, and sometimes enigmatic, and all while Astrophil protests his plainness and simplicity; the tone is aristocratic and masterful, perhaps most when Astrophil mentions his utter subjection to Stella; and line after line reads like 'a moment's thought'[2] in the very instant of betraying, or even flaunting, its conscious artistry. *Astrophil and Stella* was written for an audience that saw, not mere affectation as opposed to something vaguely called 'sincerity', but a fine regard for the dignity of man in the careful choice of armour made by Amphialus in the *New Arcadia*:

. . . he furnished him selfe for the fight: but not in his wonted furniture. For now (as if he would turne his inside outwarde) he would needes

8. Yeats, 'A Prayer for Old Age', op. cit., p. 326.
9. See above, pp. 24-5.
1. *F.Q.* III.xi.32, Spenser, p. 203.
2. Yeats, 'Adam's Curse', op. cit., p. 88.

appeare all in blacke; his decking both for him selfe, and horse, being cut out into the fashion of very ragges: yet all so dainty, joyned together with pretious stones, as it was a brave raggednesse, and a riche povertie: and so cunningly had a workeman followed his humour in his armour, that he had given it a rustie shewe, and yet so, as any man might perceive was by arte, and not negligence; carying at one instant a disgraced handsomnesse, and a new oldnes.[3]

3. Feuillerat, ed. cit., i, 454.

Bibliography

The place of publication is London, unless stated otherwise. Where more than one date is mentioned, the later date is that of the edition used.

1. Bibliography

TANNENBAUM, S. A., *Sir Philip Sidney: A Concise Bibliography*. New York, 1941.

2. Editions of Sidney

CRAIK, T. W. (ed.), *Sir Philip Sidney: Selected Poetry and Prose*. 1965.

FEUILLERAT, ALBERT (ed.), *The Complete Works of Sir Philip Sidney*, i (*The Countesse of Pembrokes Arcadia*). Cambridge, 1939 (first edition 1912).

FLÜGEL, EWALD (ed.), *Sir Philip Sidney's Astrophel and Stella und Defence of Poesie*. Halle, 1889.

GENTILI, VANNA (ed.), *Sir Philip Sidney: Astrophil and Stella*. Bari, 1965.

GROSART, A. B. (ed.), *The Complete Poems of Sir Philip Sidney*, i. 1873.

POIRIER, MICHEL, ed. and trans. into French, *Sir Philip Sidney: Astrophel and Stella*. Paris, 1957.

RATHMELL, J. C. A. (ed.), *The Psalms of Sir Philip Sidney and the Countess of Pembroke*. New York, 1963.

RINGLER, W. A. (ed.), *The Poems of Sir Philip Sidney*. Oxford, 1962.

SHEPHERD, GEOFFREY (ed.), *An Apology for Poetry*. 1965.

WILSON, MONA (ed.), *Astrophel and Stella*. 1931.

3. Anthologies containing poems by Sidney

BULLETT, GERALD (ed.), *Silver Poets of the Sixteenth Century*. 1947.

FELLOWES, E. H. (ed.), revised and enlarged by F. W. Sternfeld and David Greer, *English Madrigal Verse 1588–1632*. Oxford, 1967 (first edition 1920).

INGLIS, FRED (ed.), *English Poetry 1550–1660*. 1965.

LEE, SIDNEY (ed.), *Elizabethan Sonnets, Newly Arranged and Indexed*, i. 1904.

RUSKIN, JOHN (ed.), 'Rock Honeycomb' in *Works*, xxxi. 1907.

4. Studies of Sidney

BOAS, F. S., *Sir Philip Sidney, Representative Elizabethan: His Life and Writings.* 1955.

BUXTON, JOHN, *Sir Philip Sidney and the English Renaissance.* 1954.

COOPER, S. M., *The Sonnets of Astrophel and Stella: A Stylistic Study.* The Hague, 1968.

VAN DORSTEN, J. A., *Poets, Patrons, and Professors: Sir Philip Sidney, Daniel Rogers, and the Leiden Humanists.* 1962.

GREVILLE, SIR FULKE, LORD BROOKE, *Sir Fulke Greville's Life of Sir Philip Sidney, etc.*, Nowell Smith (ed.). Oxford, 1907.

HOWELL, ROGER, *Sir Philip Sidney: The Shepherd Knight.* 1968.

KALSTONE, DAVID, *Sidney's Poetry: Contexts and Interpretations.* Cambridge, Mass., 1965.

MONTGOMERY, R. L., *Symmetry and Sense: The Poetry of Sir Philip Sidney.* Austin, Texas, 1961.

MUIR, KENNETH, *Sir Philip Sidney.* 1967 (first edition 1960).

MYRICK, K. O., *Sir Philip Sidney as a Literary Craftsman.* Cambridge, Mass., 1935.

POIRIER, MICHEL, *Sir Philip Sidney, Le Chevalier Poète Élizabéthain.* Lille, 1948.

PURCELL, J. M., *Sidney's Stella.* 1934.

RUDENSTINE, N. L., *Sidney's Poetic Development.* Cambridge, Mass., 1967.

SYMONDS, J. A., *Sir Philip Sidney.* 1886.

WALLACE, M. W., *The Life of Sir Philip Sidney.* Cambridge, 1915.

WILSON, MONA, *Sir Philip Sidney.* 1931.

5. Essays, studies, and articles in periodicals

ANON., 'High Erected Thoughts', *T.L.S.*, 6 January 1966, p. 5.

APPLEGATE, JAMES, 'Sidney's Classical Metres', *M.L.N.* lxx (1955), 254-5.

ASCHAM, ROGER, 'Of Imitation', *Elizabethan Critical Essays*, G. Gregory Smith (ed.) (1904), i, 5-45.

AUDEN, W. H., Introduction to *William Shakespeare: The Sonnets*, William Burto (ed.). New York, 1964.

BANKS, T. H., 'Sidney's *Astrophel and Stella* Reconsidered', *P.M.L.A.* l (1935), 403-12.

BAUGHAN, D. E., 'Sir Philip Sidney and the Matchmakers', *M.L.R.* xxxiii (1938), 506-19.

BOND, W. H., 'Sidney and Cupid's Dart', *M.L.N.* lxiii (1948), 258.

BULLITT, J. M., 'The Use of Rhyme Link in the Sonnets of Sidney, Drayton, and Spenser', *J.E.G.P.* xlix (1950), 14-32.

BURHANS, C. S., 'Sidney's *With how sad steps, o Moon*', *Explicator*, xviii (1959–60), Article 26.

BUXTON, JOHN, Review of Montgomery, *R.E.S.*, N.S. xiv (1963), 99–100.

—— Review of Ringler, ibid., N.S. xv (1964), 199–202.

CASTLEY, J. P., '*Astrophel and Stella*—"High Sidnaean Love" or Courtly Compliment?', *M.C.R.*, no. 5 (1962), 54–65.

COMBELLACK, C. R. B., and ESSIG, E. H., 'Sidney's *With how sad steps, o Moon*', *Explicator*, xx (1961–2), Article 25.

COWAN, S. A., and DUDLEY, F. A., 'Sidney's *Astrophel and Stella*, IX', ibid. xx (1961–2), Article 76.

DUHAMEL, P. A., 'Sidney's *Arcadia* and Elizabethan Rhetoric', *S.P.* xlv (1948), 134–50.

DUNCAN-JONES, KATHERINE, Review of Kalstone, *R.E.S.*, N.S. xvii (1966), 457.

FLETCHER, J. B., 'Did "Astrophel" love "Stella"?', *M.P.* v (1907–8), 253–64.

FORREST, J. F., 'Bunyan's Ignorance and the Flatterer: A Study in the Literary Art of Damnation', *S.P.* lx (1963), 12–22.

FRIEDRICH, W. G., 'The Stella of Astrophel', *E.L.H.* iii (1936), 114–39.

GRUNDY, J., Review of Ringler, *M.L.R.* lviii (1963), 551–2.

HALPERN, MARTIN, 'On the Two Chief Metrical Modes in English', *P.M.L.A.* lxxvii (1962), 177–86.

HAMILTON, A. C., 'Et in Arcadia Ego', *M.L.Q.* xxvii (1966), 332–50.

—— 'The Modern Study of Renaissance English Literature: A Critical Survey', ibid. xxvi (1965), 150–83.

—— 'Sidney and Agrippa', *R.E.S.*, N.S. vii (1956), 151–7.

—— 'Sidney's *Astrophel and Stella* as a Sonnet Sequence', *E.L.H.* xxxvi (1969), 59–87.

—— 'Sidney's Idea of the "Right Poet" ', *C.L.* ix (1957), 51–9.

HOFFMAN, D. G., 'Sidney's *Thou blind man's mark*', *Explicator*, viii (1949–50), Article 29.

HOLLANDER, JOHN, 'The Music of Poetry', *J.A.A.C.* xv (1956), 232–44.

HOLLOWELL, B. M., 'The Elizabethan Hexametrists', *P.Q.* iii (1924), 51–7.

HOWE, A. R., '*Astrophel and Stella*: "Why and How" ', *S.P.* lxi (1964), 150–69.

HUDSON, H. H., 'Penelope Devereux as Sidney's Stella', *H.L.B.*, no. 7 (1935), 89–129.

HUNTER, G. K., 'Humanism and Courtship', *Elizabethan Poetry. Modern Essays in Criticism*, P. J. Alpers (ed.). Oxford, 1967, pp. 3–40.

KALSTONE, DAVID, 'Sir Philip Sidney and "Poore *Petrarchs* long deceased woes" ', *J.E.G.P.* lxiii (1964), 21–32.

LAMB, CHARLES, 'Some Sonnets of Sir Philip Sidney', *The Prose Works of Charles Lamb* (1835), iii, 138–52.

LEE, SIDNEY, 'The Elizabethan Sonnet', *The Cambridge History of English Literature*, A. W. Ward and A. R. Waller (eds.). Cambridge, 1909., iii, 247–72.

—— *Great Englishmen of the Sixteenth Century.* 1907 (first edition 1904), pp. 95–152.

LEMMI, C. W., 'Italian Borrowings in Sidney', *M.L.N.* xlii (1927), 77–9.

LYLES, A. M., 'A Note on Sidney's Use of Chaucer', *N.Q.* cxcviii (1953), 99–100.

MONTGOMERY, R. L., 'Reason, Passion, and Introspection in *Astrophel and Stella*', *T.S.E.* xxxvi (1957), 127–40.

MUIR, KENNETH, ' "Astrophel and Stella", XXXI', *N.Q.*, n.s. vii (1960), 51–2.

—— Review of Ringler, *R.N.* xvi (1963), 231–2.

MURPHY, K. M., 'The 109th and 110th Sonnets of *Astrophel and Stella*', *P.Q.* xxxiv (1955), 349–52.

NASHE, THOMAS, Preface to *Astrophel and Stella* (first Newman edition of 1591), *Elizabethan Critical Essays*, G. Gregory Smith (ed.) (1904), ii. 223–8.

PETTET, E. C., 'Sidney and the Cult of Romantic Love', *English*, vi (1946–7), 232–40.

POIRIER, MICHEL, 'Quelques Sources des Poèmes de Sidney', *E.A.* xi (1958), 150–4.

—— Review of Ringler, ibid., xvii (1964), 69–71.

PRINCE, F. T., 'The Sonnet from Wyatt to Shakespeare', *Elizabethan Poetry* (Stratford-upon-Avon Studies 2), J. R. Brown and Bernard Harris (eds.). 1960.

PURCELL, J. M., 'A Note on Sonnet II of *Astrophel and Stella*', *P.Q.* xi (1932), 402–3.

—— 'Sidney's *Astrophel and Stella* and Greville's *Caelica*', *P.M.L.A.* l (1935), 413–22.

PUTZEL, MAX, 'Sidney's *Astrophel and Stella*, IX', *Explicator*, xix (1960–1), Article 25.

REES, D. G., 'Italian and Italianate Poetry', *Elizabethan Poetry* (Stratford-upon-Avon Studies 2), J. R. Brown and Bernard Harris (eds.). 1960.

ROBERTSON, JEAN, 'Sir Philip Sidney and Lady Penelope Rich', *R.E.S.*, n.s. xv (1964), 296–7.

—— 'Sir Philip Sidney and his Poetry', *Elizabethan Poetry* (Stratford-upon-Avon Studies 2), J. R. Brown and Bernard Harris (eds.). 1960.

SALINGAR, L. G., 'The Elizabethan Literary Renaissance', *A Guide to English Literature*: ii. *The Age of Shakespeare*, Boris Ford (ed.). Harmondsworth, 1955, pp. 51–116.

SIEGEL, P. N., 'A Suggested Emendation for One of Sidney's Sonnets', *N.Q.* cxciv (1949), 75–6.

SMITH, HALLETT, 'English Metrical Psalms in the Sixteenth Century and their Literary Significance', *H.L.Q.* ix (1945–6), 249–71.

SPENCER, THEODORE, 'The Poetry of Sir Philip Sidney', *E.L.H.* xii (1945), 251–78.

STILLINGER, JACK, 'The Biographical Problem of *Astrophel and Stella*', *J.E.G.P.* lix (1960), 617–39.

—— Review of Ringler, ibid. lxii (1963), 372–8.

STROUP, T. B., 'The "Speaking Picture" Realised: Sidney's 45th Sonnet', *P.Q.* xxix (1950), 440–2.

SUDDARD, S. J. M., '*Astrophel and Stella*', *Keats, Shelley and Shakespeare. Studies and Essays in English Literature.* Cambridge, 1912, pp. 162–76.

THOMAS, DYLAN, 'Sir Philip Sidney', *Quite Early One Morning.* 1961 (first published 1954), pp. 112–21.

THOMPSON, JOHN, 'Sir Philip and the Forsaken Iamb', *K.R.* xx (1958), 90–115.

THOMSON, PATRICIA, Review of Kalstone, *M.L.R.* lxi (1966), 486–7.

TILLOTSON, GEOFFREY, 'Elizabethan Decoration', *Essays in Criticism and Research.* Cambridge, 1942, pp. 5–16.

WALTER, J. H., '*Astrophel and Stella* and *The Romaunt of the Rose*', *R.E.S.* xv (1939), 265–73.

WHIGAM, R. G., and EMERSON, O. F., 'Sonnet Structure in Sidney's "Astrophel and Stella" ', *S.P.* xviii (1921), 347–52.

WILLCOCK, G. D., 'Passing Pitefull Hexameters: A Study of Quantity and Accent in English Renaissance Verse', *M.L.R.* xxix (1934), 1–19.

WILLIAMSON, GEORGE, 'The Convention of *The Extasie*', *Seventeenth Century Contexts.* 1960, pp. 63–77.

WINTERS, YVOR, 'The Sixteenth Century Lyric in England', an essay in three parts, *P.C.* (February, March, April 1939), 258–72, 320–35, 35–51.

YATES, F. A., 'Elizabethan Chivalry: The Romance of the Accession Day Tilts', *J.W.C.I.* xx (1957), 4–25.

YOUNG, R. B., 'English Petrarke. A Study of Sidney's *Astrophel and Stella*', *Three Studies in the Renaissance: Sidney, Jonson, Milton.* New Haven, 1958, pp. 5–88.

6. Other works

AUDEN, W. H., *About the House.* 1966.

—— *Collected Shorter Poems 1927–1957.* 1966.

BERNE, ERIC, *Games People Play: The Psychology of Human Relationships.* Harmondsworth, 1968 (first published 1964).

Book of Common Prayer, The.

BRADBROOK, M. C., *Shakespeare and Elizabethan Poetry: A Study of his Earlier Work in Relation to the Poetry of the Time.* 1964 (first published 1951).

BROADBENT, J. B., *Poetic Love.* 1964.

BUNYAN, JOHN, *The Pilgrim's Progress*, Roger Sharrock (ed.). Harmondsworth, 1965.

BUXTON, JOHN, *Elizabethan Taste.* 1963.

—— *A Tradition of Poetry.* 1967.

CASTIGLIONE, BALDESAR, *The Book of the Courtier*, Sir Thomas Hoby, trans. (1561), W. E. Henley (ed.). 1900.

—— *The Book of the Courtier*, George Bull (trans.). Harmondsworth, 1967.

CATULLUS, *The Poems of Catullus*, with introduction by Robert Rowland, James Michie (ed. and trans.). 1969.

CLARK, D. L., *Rhetoric and Poetry in the Renaissance: A Study of Rhetorical Terms in English Renaissance Literary Criticism.* New York, 1963.

CRAIG, HARDIN, *The Enchanted Glass: The Elizabethan Mind in Literature.* New York, 1936.

CRANE, W. G., *Wit and Rhetoric in the Renaissance: The Formal Basis of Elizabethan Prose Style.* Gloucester, Mass., 1964 (first published 1937).

DANBY, J. F., *Elizabethan and Jacobean Poets.* 1965 (first published 1952 as *Poets on Fortune's Hill*).

DANIEL, SAMUEL, *Poems and A Defence of Ryme*, A. C. Sprague (ed.). 1950.

DRAYTON, MICHAEL, *Poems of Michael Drayton*, i, John Buxton (ed.). 1953.

EMPSON, WILLIAM, *Seven Types of Ambiguity.* Harmondsworth, 1961 (first published 1930).

EVANS, MAURICE, *English Poetry in the Sixteenth Century.* 1967 (first edition 1955).

FRAUNCE, ABRAHAM, *The Arcadian Rhetorike*, Ethel Seaton (ed.). Oxford, 1950.

FREEMAN, ROSEMARY, *Edmund Spenser.* 1962 (first edition 1957).

GASCOIGNE, GEORGE, *The Complete Works of George Gascoigne*, i, J. W. Cunliffe (ed.). Cambridge, 1907.

GREAVES, MARGARET, *The Blazon of Honour: A Study in Renaissance Magnanimity.* 1964.

GREVILLE, SIR FULKE, LORD BROOKE, *Selected Poems of Fulke Greville*, Thom Gunn (ed.). 1968.

HAMILTON, A. C., *The Structure of Allegory in The Faerie Queene.* Oxford, 1964 (first published 1961).

HERBERT, GEORGE, *The Works of George Herbert*, F. E. Hutchinson (ed.). Oxford, 1941.

Holy Bible, The. Geneva Version. 1594 (first published 1560).

—— Revised Standard Version. 1961 (first published 1952).

HOSKINS, JOHN, *Directions for Speech and Style*, H. H. Hudson (ed.). Princeton, 1935.

INGLIS, FRED, *The Elizabethan Poets: The Making of English Poetry from Wyatt to Ben Jonson*. 1969.

JOHN, L. C., *The Elizabethan Sonnet Sequences: Studies in Conventional Conceits*. New York, 1938.

JONSON, BEN, *Ben Jonson*, viii, C. H. Herford and Percy and Evelyn Simpson (eds.). Oxford, 1947.

LEVER, J. W., *The Elizabethan Love Sonnet*. 1966 (first published 1956).

LEWIS, C. S., *The Allegory of Love: A Study in Medieval Tradition*. Oxford, 1953 (first edition 1936).

—— *English Literature in the Sixteenth Century, Excluding Drama*, vol. iii of *The Oxford History of English Literature*. Oxford, 1962 (first published 1954).

MARTZ, L. L., *The Poetry of Meditation: A Study in English Religious Literature of the Seventeenth Century*. New Haven, 1955 (first published 1954).

MILLER, E. H., *The Professional Writer in Elizabethan England: A Study of Nondramatic Literature*. Cambridge, Mass., 1959.

MILTON, JOHN, *Milton's Sonnets*, E. A. J. Honigmann (ed.). 1966.

MOORE, MARIANNE, *Collected Poems*. New York, 1951.

DE MOURGUES, ODETTE, *Metaphysical, Baroque, and Précieux Poetry*. Oxford, 1953.

MUIR, KENNETH, *Introduction to Elizabethan Literature*. New York, 1967.

NELSON, WILLIAM, *The Poetry of Edmund Spenser*. New York, 1965 (first published 1963).

Oxford English Dictionary, The. Oxford, 1961 (first published 1933).

PETERSON, D. L., *The English Lyric from Wyatt to Donne: A History of the Plain and Eloquent Styles*. Princeton, 1967.

RALEGH, SIR WALTER, *The Poems of Sir Walter Ralegh*, Agnes Latham (ed.). London, 1962 (first published 1951).

RENWICK, W. L., *Edmund Spenser: An Essay on Renaissance Poetry*. 1925.

RUBEL, V. L., *Poetic Diction in the English Renaissance, from Skelton through Spenser*. New York, 1941.

SALOMON, L. B., *The Devil Take Her! A Study of the Rebellious Lover in English Poetry*. New York, 1961 (first published 1931).

SCOTT, J. G., *Les Sonnets Élisabéthains: Les Sources et l'Apport Personnel*. Paris, 1929.

SHAKESPEARE, WILLIAM, *King Lear*, Kenneth Muir (ed.). 1955 (first published 1952).

—— *The Sonnets*, J. Dover Wilson (ed.). Cambridge, 1966.

SMITH, HALLETT, *Elizabethan Poetry: A Study in Conventions, Meaning and Expression*. Cambridge, Mass., 1952.

SONNINO, L. A., *A Handbook to Sixteenth-Century Rhetoric*. 1968.

SPENSER, EDMUND, *The Mutabilitie Cantos*, S. P. Zitner (ed.). 1968.

—— *The Poetical Works of Edmund Spenser*, J. C. Smith and E. de Selincourt (eds.). Oxford, 1940 (first published 1912).

—— *The Works of Edmund Spenser: A Variorum Edition*, vi, Edwin Greenlaw, C. G. Osgood, F. M. Padelford, Ray Heffner, J. G. McManaway, D. E. Mason, Brents Stirling (eds.). Baltimore, 1961 (first published 1938).

STRONG, ROY, *The Elizabethan Image: Painting in England 1540–1620*. Catalogue of exhibition at the Tate Gallery, 28 November 1969–8 February 1970.

TALON, H. A., *John Bunyan*. 1964 (first edition 1956).

TENNYSON, ALFRED, *The Poems of Tennyson*, Christopher Ricks (ed.). 1969.

THOMPSON, JOHN, *The Founding of English Metre*. New York, 1961.

TILLEY, M. P., *A Dictionary of the Proverbs in England in the Sixteenth and Seventeenth Centuries*. Ann Arbor, 1950.

TUVE, ROSEMOND, *Elizabethan and Metaphysical Imagery*. Chicago, 1965 (first edition 1947).

VIRGIL. *Virgil*, i, H. H. Fairclough (trans.). 1965.

WIND, EDGAR, *Pagan Mysteries in the Renaissance*. Harmondsworth, 1967 (first edition 1958).

YEATS, W. B., *Collected Poems*. 1950.

General index

allegory, 39–42, 92–3, 99
alliteration, 36, 73, 137, 142, 149
allusions, 37, 82, 97, 99, 129;
    heraldic, 86–7, 94, 98–9
ambiguity, 6, 141–2, 151
artifice, 24, 61, 102, 137
Ascham, Roger, 'Of imitation',
    13–14, 17–18
Auden, W. H., *About the House*,
    16 n.; 'The truest poetry is the
    most feigning', 89, 127
audiences, 24, 40–1, 65–6, 95, 127–9,
    134–5, 153

Banks, T. H., 'Sidney's *Astrophel
    and Stella* reconsidered', 62
Berne, Eric, *Games People Play*, 133
biographical intrusion, 53–9, 62, 65,
    77–8, 85–90, 93–7, 124, 133
Blount, Sir Charles (later Lord
    Mountjoy), 57, 97 n.
Boas, F. S., *Sir Philip Sidney and the
    English Renaissance*, 66
Book of Common Prayer, 21
Botticelli, *Birth of Venus*, 145
Broadbent, J. B., *Poetic Love*, 130
Bull, George, *The Book of the
    Courtier* (1967), 9
Bunyan, John, *Pilgrim's Progress*,
    92–3

Castiglione, Baldesar, *Il libro del
    cortegiano* (1528), 8
Catullus, 52, 59; poems, 53
charm, 10, 34, 41, 59
classical myth, 37–41
climax, 143, 144

compliment, 20, 32, 62, 96, 100,
    101, 132–4, 146–8
conflict, 105–10, 112, 115, 122
Craig, Hardin, *The Enchanted Glass*, 19

Daniel, Samuel, 10
Devereux, Penelope, 52, 61, 62, 66;
    see also Rich
Devereux, Robert, Earl of Essex
    (d. 1601), 97 n.; arms, 86, 99
'dialettica dell'ostacolo', 106
diction, 137
drama, 46–8, 66–7, 70–2, 77–8,
    80–1, 87, 104, 111–12, 123, 136
Drayton, Michael, 10

Edward IV, of England, 148, 149,
    150
Elizabeth I, of England, 10, 24
eloquence, 54, 71, 81
Essex, Earl of, *see* Devereux, Robert

fiction, 7, 42, 44–5, 61, 65, 77,
    81–3, 87, 89, 91–3, 127
Fraunce, Abraham, *The Arcadian
    Rhetorike*, 22–3
Friedrich, W. G., 'The Stella of
    Astrophel', 63–4 n.

Gascoigne, George, 'Certayne notes
    of Instruction . . .', 6; 'Gascoigne's
    woodmanship', 138
Gentili, Vanna, *Sir Philip Sidney . . .*,
    60, 64 n., 143
Gifford, George, 'The Manner of Sir
    Philip Sidney's Death', 62–3
Gonzago, Hannibal, Spanish
    commander, 12 n.

puns, 5, 26
Purcell, J. M., *Sidney's Stella*, 61–2

quantitative verse, 13–16

Ralegh, Sir Walter, 10; epitaph on
    Sidney, 12
rhetoric, 8, 22–3, 25–7, 36, 141, 142
rhyme, 12, 28, 78, 114, 137, 140–1,
    149
rhythm, 28, 99, 137, 140, 145, 147
Rich, Penelope, Lady Rich, 52, 56,
    57, 62–6, 78, 85, 87, 94, 97 n.,
    133–4; *see also* Devereux
Rich, Robert, Lord Rich (d. 1619),
    56, 62, 64–5, 66, 90, 96–7
Ringler, W. J., *The Poems of Sir
    Philip Sidney*, 121
Robertson, Jean, 'Sir Philip Sidney
    and Lady Penelope Rich', 62
Rudenstine, N. L., *Sidney's Poetic
    Development*, 104
Ruskin, John, 'Rock Honeycomb',
    49

Shakespeare, William, 11, 111, 121;
    sonnets, 10 n., 33–4, 35–6, 50
Sidney, Sir Henry, Lord Deputy of
    Ireland, 78, 85, 90
Sidney, Sir Philip, 8–11, 52, 61, 66,
    78, 81, 90, 152; arms, 86, 94;
    epitaph, 12; sister, *see* Herbert,
    Mary; wife, *see* Walsingham,
    Frances
    Apology for Poetry, 2, 6, 13, 43, 46,
    53, 62, 73, 85, 92, 131, 144;
    extracts, 7, 8, 19, 25–6, 38–9,
    40, 44–5, 89, 104, 152; *New
    Arcadia*, 75; extracts, 50,
    153–4; *Psalms of David*, 48–9
poetic works, *see* Index of first lines
Siegel, P. N., 'A Suggested
    Emendation . . .', 19 n.
sincerity, 53–4, 66
Skelton, John, 53
songs, 120–7
sonnets, 4, 10, 27, 33–6, 81,
    114–15, 130, 136

sonnet sequences, 52, 61, 65–6,
    112–17, 120, 136
Spenser, Edmund, 10, 45, 114;
    Amoretti, 144; *Colin Clouts Come
    Home Againe*, 90, 131; *
    Epithalamium*, 150 n.; *Faerie
    Queene*, 11, 35, 40, 42–3, 75–6,
    90–1, 92, 153; *Mutabilitie Cantos*,
    114 n.; *Shepheardes Calender*, 25
sprezzatura, 9
stress, 137–8; *see also* quantitative
    verse
Strong, Roy, *The Elizabethan Image*,
    130 n.
subtlety, 3, 87
symmetry, 23, 35
Symonds, J. A., *Sir Philip Sidney*,
    56, 70

Tennyson, Alfred, Lord, 16
themes, 72, 77, 116–17, 120, 123,
    146
Thomas, Dylan, 'Sir Philip Sidney',
    59–60, 131–2
tone, 4, 137
Tuve, Rosemond, *Elizabethan and
    Metaphysical Imagery*, 27

Virgil, 23; *Aeneid*, 40
virtue, 67–9, 73–9, 148

Wallace, M. W., *Life of Sir Philip
    Sidney*, 56, 58
Walsingham, Frances, 54, 97 n.
Williamson, George, 'The
    Convention of *The Exstasie*', 48
Wilson, Mona, *Sir Philip Sidney*, 54
Winters, Yvor, 'The Sixteenth
    Century Lyric in England', 48
wit, 2, 6, 31, 73, 81, 88, 146–8,
    150, 151, 153

Yeats, W. B., 'A Prayer for Old
    Age', 153
Young, R. B., 'English
    Petrarke . . .', 4, 72

Zutphen, battle of (1586), 9, 12 n.

Index of first lines

Songs

Doubt you to whom my Muse these notes entendeth (1), 28–9, 101 n., 117 n., 122, 140

Go my flocke, go get you hence (9), 13, 40 n., 109 n., 110 n., 121 n., 124–5, 127

Have I caught my heavn'ly jewell (2), 55, 109, 120 n., 122–3

If Orpheus' voyce had force to breathe such musicke's love (3), 38 n., 123

In a grove most rich of shade (8), 48, 56, 65, 93, 95, 96, 106 n., 109 n., 110 n., 121 and n. 4, 124, 125

O deare life, when shall it be (10), 65, 110 n., 120 n., 125–6
Onely joy, now here you are (4), 56, 106 n., 109, 121 and n. 4, 123–4, 126
O you that heare this voice (6), 121 and n. 8, 124

While favour fed my hope, delight with hope was brought (5), 101 n., 102, 120 n., 121 and n. 8, 123, 124
Who is it that this darke night (11), 65, 110 n., 120 n., 126–7, 131 n.
Whose senses in so evill consort, their stepdame Nature laies (7), 117 n., 121 and n. 8, 124

CERTAIN SONNETS

Leave me ô Love, which reachest but to dust (32), 21–2, 36 n., 57–8

My mistresse lowers and saith I do not love (17), 20

Oft have I musde, but now at length I finde (20), 29
O my thoughtes' sweete foode, my, my onely owner (5), 68

The Nightingale, as soone as Aprill bringeth (4), 1, 2, 45 n., 88–9
Thou blind man's marke, thou foole's self chosen snare (31), 35, 36, 57–8, 141

OLD ARCADIA

And are you there old Pas? in troth I ever thought (29), 3
A neighbor mine not long agoe there was (64), 3, 42, 43, 46
As I my little flocke on Ister banke (66), 41, 46

Come Dorus, come, let songs thy sorowes signifie (7), 26

In faith, good Histor, long is your delay (67), 47 n.